HOMEMADE BOOKS TO HELP KIDS COPE

< >

An Easy-to-Learn Technique for Parents and Professionals

ROBERT G. ZIEGLER, M.D.

Magination Press • Washington, DC

A NOTE ON PRONOUNS: To avoid such awkward constructions as "he or she," "her/him," and "s/he," all pronouns referring to *child,* unless the text specifies one sex or the other, are feminine in odd-numbered chapters, masculine in even-numbered ones. Pronouns referring to *parent,* however, are the other way around.

Library of Congress Cataloging-in-Publication Data

Ziegler, Robert G.
    Homemade books to help kids cope : an easy-to-learn technique for
parents and professionals / Robert G. Ziegler.
        p.   cm.
    ISBN 0-945354-50-9
    1. Child psychology. 2. Children's stories – Authorship.
3. Bibliotherapy for children. 4. Parenting. I. Title.
HQ772.Z54 1992
649'.58 – dc20   92-28750
                                                      CIP

Published by Magination Press, an imprint of the Educational Publishing Foundation, American Psychological Association, 750 First Street, NE, Washington, DC 20002.

Manufactured in the United States of America
10 9 8 7 6 5

This book is dedicated

to   my children, Lisa and Jeffrey, for whom my first storybooks were written to help manage a troublesome moment or a life event, and to their mother, Patricia, without whom all of it would have been impossible;

to   all those who encouraged the creation of stories to help their children or other children they knew: Sally Benbasset and Steve Miller, Emily Schatzow and Charlie Deutsch, Joan and John Daly, Jan Naegele and Paul Lombroso, Gail and Walter Willett, Nina Masters, and other parents and grandparents of children who have prompted my search for new ways to help children; and

to   the staff of Eliot Clinic's Therapeutic Primary Program, including Mady Drucker, Laura Englander, Judy Hanselman, Anne McGloin, Sheri Madden, and JoAnn Silverman, who, through the years, have supported and nurtured my work with children of all ages.

Contents

List of Stories

*illustrated

*illustrated

Introduction

I first discovered the value of writing stories with kids at home as I helped my own children deal with changes, feelings, and unexpected events in our lives. I learned that when I told them about something new (bad or otherwise), they often forgot important aspects of what I said or became confused about details. I realized they needed an opportunity to "see" what I was saying. This led to the natural conclusion that if I made them a book, they could *see* the parts of each event in their own story, and they could also *hear* the story over and over again. Reading it together could provide us both with the warmth of a very special exchange.

Then, in my work as a child psychiatrist with preschool teachers, in both normal nurseries and therapeutic preschools, I began to create stories for teachers to read to children. Finally, in my private practice with younger children and their families, I found this technique tremendously helpful.

Little by little, in order to help with various difficult situations they had to face, I wrote storybooks for children between the ages of two and eleven. I then began to experiment with how to use this technique with adolescents. The book you now have in your hand was written as an extension of all this work, to show parents, teachers, and counselors how to develop stories to help guide children through new or troublesome events.

Using stories to teach about life's experiences and human feelings is scarcely an original idea. Whether around an open fire, as in earlier cultures, or in a big armchair today, story-telling can help everyone, old and young, to deal with many different worries. Folklore, religious parables, and legends have shown people their particular niche in the world. Stories have taught us how to consider solutions for typical human conflicts. Whether they relate the adventures of talking animals, of fictitious characters, or of historical figures, stories have always offered both a sense of hope and possible pathways to follow.

WHO CAN USE THIS BOOK?

Parents, teachers, and counselors all look for ways to give children hope as well as better understanding.

Parents. Parents can use these ideas to help children in a wide variety of situations. In addition, the fun of "figuring life out together" solidifies the bond between parent and child in a very special way.

Teachers. Teachers often gain access to children's problems in ways that other adults do not. This technique is compatible with other educational approaches and demonstrates the importance of reading, writing, and self-expression.

Child Counselors and Therapists. Many counselors in family-based agencies, school systems, or child guidance centers can use story-making as part of a multifaceted approach to the difficulties of the children they see. Therapists in private practice will also find this technique helpful.

Whichever category you fall into, your use of this book should be tailored to your needs. For many parents, it may be a resource you have sought because of a specific problem you are facing with your child. In that case, I advise reading the first three chapters, then going straight on to whatever section seems most appropriate. Parents, especially, know the particular language their children use to label what they are experiencing and are witness to the many feelings that accompany change. Homemade books can help children to improve their ability to manage change, in the loving context of storytime.

WHAT THIS BOOK IS ABOUT

Chapter 1 introduces three basic types of books that can be written for a child. They are books that: 1) describe the situation; 2) define the child's feelings; and/or 3) make a general and empathic statement.

Children, like adults, prefer change in small doses. Even a happy event (like a trip) is made happier through fantasy and anticipation. Stories about events reduce their size and shape to fit a child's understanding. For most young children, the changes parents will want to describe are normal life events. Everyday stories, such as are described in Chapter 2, can be written to help a child cope with the stress brought about by such changes, and even to welcome them.

Chapter 3 describes illustration techniques and how to adjust the level of complexity in the book to the age of the child.

The pressures in two-career or single-parent families require additional dialogue. Busy schedules in any family generate tension and a sense of neglect. Chapter 4 describes how to make books that focus on such feelings. Upsetting moments, angry exchanges, or conflicting emotions can be made into stories that can assist the whole family to reconsider difficult times. Reading them together emphasizes the support that parents offer their children.

Chapter 5 explains how to write longer stories. Parents will learn how to gather information and to think about common changes (like new siblings, moves, or schools) in the child's situation that become permanent or will last an extended period of time. Longer stories can also be used to help children review accomplishments or events in the past year. Giving children perspective about time and the connections among multiple events helps them to grow in understanding.

Chapter 6 shows how to write stories for children as they face various developmental steps—from giving up a bottle to facing the confusions of puberty. It discusses how to enrich the dialogue between yourself and your child, so that the normal hesitations experienced in growing older do not become blocks to healthy development. Behavioral management techniques can be spelled out and reinforced. Transitions, like those demanded by a family's move and altered schedules, are also reviewed here.

Chapter 7 discusses the family as a source of comfort and support during times of illness or loss. It stresses speaking to a child's particular feelings about a painful life event. If adversity strikes a family member, the information and the feelings can be put into a book to help the child cope.

Chapter 8 focuses on another difficult time of life. Children need special attention when parents divorce, and a home-made book can relate the consequences in a step-by-step fashion.

Chapter 9 shows how, as part of the adoption process, a book can make it easier for children to integrate their past histories with their present families. It also shows how to create a book to help a child through parental illness or injury.

In Chapter 10, new adaptations are encouraged. Stories can help children find new ways to approach situations so they do not repeat familiar (perhaps troublesome) roles over and over. For example, a story can show a shy child how to act in unfamiliar situations or an awkward child how to be more confident. A "book about me" can help a child to try something new or can reinforce fresh starts.

The last chapter explores how to overcome some hitches that might be encountered in the process of making storybooks.

Homemade books, like any others, can be read over and over. Since they are made-to-order, they can be modified whenever necessary. Children do not usually understand something after only one explanation, and sometimes it is hard to know what most confuses them. By making a storybook, parents create an opportunity for their child to ask questions that the parents might never have been able to anticipate.

Books also help children (as they do adults) pick up and put down their challenges in life. A book can be closed and the associated emotions turned off before the child is over-whelmed. Children and parents can always return to the page and try again. Often, after having been read to, children will sit alone with the book and repeat the story to themselves. Once they have heard their own stories, children can benefit more easily from other "real-life" books, such as *My First Day at School,* or *The Boys' and Girls' Book About Divorce,* or *I'm Going to the Hospital Today.* They will learn that hard times, and the feelings associated with them, happen to others as well.

Some parents may feel it is best to avoid stressful news. The arrival of the babysitter or the trip to the doctor may be kept a secret; Daddy's or Mommy's temper may never be mentioned. Time and again, though, childcare experts have found that reviewing the problem helps the child cope, even if difficult feelings are aroused. It is better to talk with your child about how bad it feels to be left with a babysitter than to face a temper tantrum when you are sneaking out the door. Such discussions may make children sad or angry momentarily, but reactions are worse when they feel betrayed by not being informed or when their perceptions and emotions are denied. Making stories about scary and problematic as well as simple life events reassures children that their parents will protect them from mystery and fear with knowledge.

While the storybooks that parents write may lack the grand adventure of a fairy tale or the romantic ending of a Hollywood movie, they can help children better understand the world they actually inhabit. Children are reminded that their own lives can be the source of good stories, too. Helpful stories written by parents can give children an opportunity to eliminate one fearsome giant (Misunderstanding) from the world, and they'll feel safer, as their faith in their parents and themselves is increased.

< 1 >

Three Basic Types of Stories

As a baby, my son Jeffrey had one ear infection after another. No matter what medicine he was given, shortly after he stopped taking it – and sometimes before – he would develop yet another infection. He suffered the pain and discomfort, while we wore thin our only carpet by pacing and rocking him to sleep in our arms. Finally, he had ear surgery. His new tubes helped prevent his problem with infections. But now we had a different problem. Jeffrey was used to extended walks and sleeping close to us (or not sleeping at all), but he now had a new bedtime routine to master. We expected him to go to bed and stay there!

I still recall the night my wife and I first steeled ourselves to sit together on the couch after we put Jeffrey in his crib. He cried, he howled. We sat. The first night, and the second, he won. We gave in. We went to him, explained again that this was a new bedtime routine, patted and comforted him until he got to sleep. On the third night, we were able to sit longer. He cried, he wailed, and then, silence. We sat holding each other's hands and waited. Had he really fallen asleep? When could we check?

Suddenly we heard his crib rattling, then a thump on the floor. We heard the padding of his little feet heading in our direction. He came into the room where we were sitting and said, "Cwying, cwying!" He was *telling* us that he was crying, since just doing it didn't seem to have the desired effect. What, the tone of his voice said, were we going to do about it?

It was a good question. He was beginning to catch on to the fact that there was a new story going on at bedtime. Things had changed. We hadn't really helped him to understand what the old story was about or what the new one would be. The old story was crying, pacing, and sitting with him until he fell asleep. The new story was a cuddle, a kiss, and falling asleep alone.

I realized Jeffrey needed a storybook to get a better idea of what was happening in his life. Let me show you what I did then. This is what I wrote:

Jeffrey's New Bedtime Story

page 1: When Jeffrey was sick, it was very hard for him to get to sleep. His ears would hurt and he would cry.
Mommy had to walk with him.
Daddy had to walk with him.
Sometimes Mommy and Daddy would sit by his bed and rub his back.
page 2: Now Jeffrey is well.
Jeffrey gets hugs and kisses. He goes to bed with his teddy.
He can listen to his special songs on his tape.
He can wave "Nite, nite!" to Mommy and Daddy.
page 3: Sometimes Jeffrey still cries when he goes to bed.
Mommy or Daddy will come in and say, "No more time for crying; it is time for sleeping."
Mommy or Daddy will give Jeffrey another pat and say "Nite, nite" again.
Jeffrey can hug his teddy and go to sleep.
NITE! NITE! Everyone!

Jeffrey loved his new book. It helped him get to sleep. It helped him remember what the new routine was. Sometimes, even during the day, he would bring it over to be read to him.

After all my training as a child therapist, I had still assumed that he would somehow just pick up this new routine after we had told him about it. We ourselves were so ready for the new routine that we forgot that children of all ages need more preparation.

BOOKS TO DESCRIBE A SITUATION

Making books for children is a natural way to prepare them for change. It helps them understand a new situation. Even small changes are made easier for both parent and child. Jeffrey's book was designed to describe a new situation in a low-key, nonjudgmental way. This is the first step. Making books is a very helpful way to introduce children to new ideas, new situations, and even family interactions. The first ones I wrote were for my daughter, when she began nursery school and, later, when a new baby (Jeffrey) was headed our way (see Chapter 4).

Writing these books helped me as a parent, too. It supplied an opportunity to stop and think about what was going on with my children. In the hustle and bustle of everyday life, even as a trained child therapist, I would find myself simply reacting. I needed some quiet time to think about what was going on. I wanted to share what I had figured out with my children. What better way than by making a story about it? Children can use the assistance of homemade books to deal with all kinds of experiences—happy, sad, scary, as well as those they normally face in the course of growing older.

I have often told parents that sometimes you have to say *no* a million times in order for a child to understand that you really-truly mean it. The message does not get through right away. Children need repetition to absorb information and to learn a new concept. Then again, is it so different for adults? Sometimes we don't really know how much stress we are under until we make a list of all the recent changes in our lives.

These days there are books to help us, as adults, with nearly every challenge imaginable: a job change, how to fix a car, recipes, a divorce, where to go with a new invention. Why not use the same idea with children? Curious George helps children with many situations and so do the Berenstain Bears, but sometimes the message you want to give your child is uniquely yours. And you, the parent, are the best person to convey it.

Our children need our help in getting the whole picture. They cannot easily understand all the elements of the story that is happening to them. The big view is provided by parents through patience and repetition. Describing a situation can be a first step, but there is a second.

BOOKS TO DEFINE FEELINGS

Children's feelings are a big part of what they experience, yet they often need help in identifying and accepting those feelings. This is another area where homemade books can help. They can help by describing children's behavior in a nonjudgmental way and by labeling feelings.

While labeling feelings is something we do naturally, as parents, for our children, sometimes we have to admit that we do not like our children's behavior, or their feelings. But, before change can happen, children, like adults, need to experience *acceptance of the situation and of the feelings as they exist.* Only with acceptance can children identify and understand their feelings.

Of course, our children challenge our ability to admit, accept, and describe their behavior in a nonjudgmental fashion. Before a mother could write the storybook called "Joshua Knows How to Make Becca Cry," her child had challenged her ability to accept his feelings.

Mother #1: I'm so glad that you came over today. I've been feeling so frustrated with Joshua lately. There was a time when he was playing so nicely with his sister, but now all he does is tease her. It seems like the only thing that happens between me and Joshua anymore is my yelling at him and telling him to go to his room and play by himself.

Mother #2: What are you yelling at him about?

Mother #1: It's what he says to his sister. Maybe he got it from kindergarten. Maybe I should go to talk to his teacher about what goes on at school. I should see if some other child is picking on him and calling him terrible names or something. Joshua always enjoyed Becca so much, even though she's three years younger. What he's doing now really bothers me.

Mother #2: What is he doing?

Mother #1: Well, I guess I should be glad he's not hitting her. We've told him over and over again, Use your words, and he certainly is. I feel like I hear those words a hundred times a day after he's home from school.

Mother #2: What is he saying?

Mother #1: It's so embarrassing. He must know that I hate it. I mean, I tell him that I do. He also knows I send him to his room for it, so why does he keep it up?

Mother #2: Don't you want to tell me what it is he's saying?

Mother #1: I guess I do, but believe me this isn't easy. Every time Becca sits down in front of him when he's watching TV, or when she picks up one of his toys, or when she gets her choice of dessert for the night, he just looks at her and says, "Becca's got boogers," and she gets upset and starts crying. I've told her to ignore him, but I can't ignore him myself. What if he acts like that in front of my mother when she visits?

Mother #2: That does sound embarrassing.

Once Joshua's mother could accept that even in his loving relationship with his little sister he could still be mad, mean, provocative, teasing, jealous, and all those other things that one doesn't like one's child to be, the stage was set for her to write a book to help him understand his feelings – and, in so doing, to diminish their intensity. Here is the book:

Joshua Knows How to Make Becca Cry

page 1: Becca is Joshua's little sister. She is three. Joshua is six and sometimes he thinks his little sister is a pest.

page 2: When Becca sits in front of Joshua while he is watching TV, he whispers, "Becca's got boogers."

page 3: When Becca picks up one of Joshua's toys, Joshua says, "Becca's got boogers."

page 4: When it is Becca's night to pick the dessert, if Joshua doesn't like it, he says, "Becca's got boogers."

page 5: Whenever Joshua gets mad, he says, "Becca's got boogers."

page 6: Sometimes, when you go off to kindergarten, it's hard to have a little sister.

Joshua was able to use this story to help him contain his anger. Soon, he was able to joke with his mother and say, "Boogers!" when he felt he was mad. Mother was able to accept this as a code word and no longer reacted as strongly. Becca got in on the act, too. Even though younger siblings will put up with a great deal in order to have the attention and affection of an older sibling, she was better able to understand that Joshua was mad from listening in on the story. It made perfect sense to her.

When a book can describe either the situation, as Jeffrey's did, or the child's behavior and feelings, as Joshua's did, it can open a path for the child to become more comfortable. This process can be facilitated by making a general closing statement that expresses empathy for the child, as that last page of Joshua's story did.

Here is another life change a mother and father had to examine.

Father: Ever since you started working one evening a week, Billy has been very uncooperative when I pick him up after school. He doesn't listen to anything I say and cries at the drop of a hat.

Mother: I've noticed that he's crying again when I drop him off at school. He hasn't done that since nursery school. He was really used to the routine last year in kindergarten, and not that much has changed.

Father: That's right. Last year he went to the same after-school program, too. Is his new teacher mean?

Mother: No, lots of Adam's friends had her and loved her. I've spoken to other mothers and they think she's fine. Adam thinks his little brother is just a spoiled brat these days.

Father: I know. If Billy isn't crying when I pick him up, Adam is sure to make him cry with some remark. But I think Adam is trying to help the little guy out, even if he is fed up with him. I checked with Billy's after-school teachers and they said he's having a lot of trouble there, too. He gets mad more easily and sometimes just withdraws from whatever they are doing.

Mother: Well, maybe I should quit my job. This has only been happening since I started it. Maybe Billy's just too young.

Father: I don't know if the answer is for us to feel guilty and rearrange our lives, but it sure seems we need to do something.

What was needed was to provide Billy with a chance to try to understand the bigger picture. Whenever changes are affecting family members, the first book made for a child should describe the situation in the simplest possible terms. Once these parents were able to put the elements of the new situation into a book, their child felt better. He could see the new situation more clearly and accept his own feelings about the changes in his family.

The Family's Week

page 1: Sunday is a day that our family is together. We plan a lot of different things to do.

page 2: Monday, Mom takes Billy and Adam to school. Dad

goes to work and picks up the kids at after-school. Mom comes home from work for supper.

page 3: Tuesday is a new kind of day. Mom drops the kids off at school, but she isn't home for supper. She has a new job. Dad makes supper with Billy and Adam. They eat supper without Mom.

page 4: Wednesday both Billy and Adam go to karate after school. Mom takes them there and brings them home. Wednesday is Daddy's late night at work so we have a snack after karate before we eat supper with Dad.

page 5: Thursday and Friday are kind of the same. Work for Mom and Dad and school for the kids.

page 6: Saturday is a busy day for everyone. Sometimes there are soccer games and sometimes we all go to the playground.

Billy and Adam's Mom and Dad could have written a book about the situation, or one that described Billy's new behavior and his feelings, or one that tried to do both. They decided, as I would recommend, to start by simply describing the situation. They did not want to describe Billy's feelings yet because he was upset so often, and that might only add to his worries. After they had read the book together for two nights, Billy went into his bedroom with crayons and paper. He said he wanted to make a new cover for their book. He came back with this one:

I HATE TOOSDAY!

Billy's cover did two things. It clarified what he was mad and sad about. It also showed how the family's book had helped him to organize his experience so that he could share his feelings in a more specific way.

Situations and feelings are often intertwined. Sometimes we can focus on the situation and clarify the feelings. At other times, by describing the feelings, we can help the child to understand the situation. Both Jeffrey and Billy needed some information pulled together about their new situations.

Joshua needed to have his behavior described to help him define his feelings so that he no longer had to intrude them into every interaction with his sister Becca.

BOOKS TO MAKE AN EMPATHIC STATEMENT

Books are a natural and comfortable way to help children (and parents) get a little distance. We may actively listen to our children, as the dialogue below illustrates, but a book can help a child gain and keep a sense of perspective. This can be accomplished through a third type of book, reaching for a general and empathic statement or conclusion, qualified by the word "sometimes."

Child (Elliot): I just don't want to go to soccer today.

Mother: Why not, honey? Last week you had a lot of fun.

Father: Your team won, too.

Child: I think it's too hot today.

Mother: Well, let's put on your shorts. They always make you feel cooler.

Child: I hate the stupid colors on our shirts and shorts.

Father: Teams have to play, whatever the weather. The Braves don't stop playing just because it's too hot. They also have to wear their uniforms, no matter what colors.

Child: I just don't want to go. Why are you being so mean? Nobody in this family likes me!

Mother: You sound really angry about having to go to soccer.

Child: I am! Johnny is really mean. He keeps hogging the ball, and he got in my way so I couldn't even make a goal. After that, the coach put me on defense. It was really boring. Then, when the team rushed the goal, he yelled at me. I hate soccer!

Father: Sometimes you wish you didn't have soccer?

Child: I hate Johnny, and the coach. I like playing, though. How come they can't be nicer?

Here is what a book might look like that could be helpful to this child:

Elliot's Team

page 1: Every Tuesday and Saturday we practice for soccer. We have our games on Saturdays. Our coach is Michael. Two of my friends, Johnny and Mark, are on the team. We're called the Golden Eagles.

page 2: The coach likes to put me on defense. It's boring when everyone else is working on getting a goal. Sometimes the game changes really fast. If you don't do what the coach wants right away, he yells. I hate his yelling.

page 3: Sometimes Johnny plays a position that I want. It makes me mad. I could play forward, too. I think the coach should have us take turns. Sometimes he does.

page 4: My favorite soccer game was against the Brown Bears. We beat them 6 to 2. I helped get the ball back to their territory and we made a goal. The coach told me I protected our lead. I felt good.

page 5: But sometimes I just hate to go to soccer. Mom and Dad drive me there anyway. They say: Sometimes it's hard to be a soccer defenseman.

Making books together can create a very tangible sense of parental involvement. While you are reading your book, there is a special companionship in which full attention is shared. Your child can tell that you really understand the situation, because you have described it in an accurate but neutral and accepting way. There are opportunities to recall feelings and to name them together without embarrassment. Children can understand that their feelings will be accepted, even while the story may suggest that certain actions must be limited. After the reading, you will find you have created a good mood for further dialogue.

The examples so far have been for younger children (from 18 months to six years). Once the basic techniques have been mastered, it will be easy to make books for older kids, whose greater knowledge and attention span permit more complexity and a larger vocabulary for both ideas and feelings. The next chapters look at how to write such stories, and at some techniques for illustrating them.

< **2** >

Stories for
Everyday Life

The first chapter helped us define some basic types of books we can make for children. Every time we make one, we are involved in an exercise in communication, and communication works best when we adjust our words to the age and understanding of the child. As children grow older, their comprehension of life situations increases, so the books we make can be more complex. They can also be more of a cooperative effort. The child's involvement can be expressed through the art work as well as the words. In Chapter 3, different ways to illustrate these books will be discussed.

First, let us see how books can be used for three everyday situations that children have to manage. These are: 1) the family's daily routine; 2) school; and 3) friendships. Children's self-esteem and self-confidence initially depend upon how we help them to master such tasks and to feel they are part of the family. (Within families feelings can run high. How children handle emotions with siblings and parents will be tackled in Chapter 4, after we have practiced with these three topics.)

A good place to begin is with a book that will help to organize your child's thinking about routines at home. It can make clear your expectations and define your hopes for how things will work.

Here are the sounds of a typical morning in many families:

Timmy (age four): Mommy, where are my shoes?

Mother: Timmy, turn off that TV, you won't find your shoes in the living room. Ask Jimmy to help you. Where did you leave them last night? I told you to keep them in the closet.

Kate (age nine): I don't want Crispy Critters this morning. Can't you make some hot oatmeal? My stomach feels cold, I don't think I can walk to school today.

Mother: Kate, you need to get up earlier, so your stomach has time to wake up. Bring your bowl over to the stove. I can use some of the hot water for my tea to make you instant oatmeal.

Father: Morning, honey, I'll just grab an egg and be out of here.

Mother: Can't you take Kate to the bus stop? She'll just be a minute after she has her oatmeal.

Jim (age 13): I can't find Timmy's shoes. And when I went to help him, he hid under the bed. When I tried pulling him out, he bumped his head. Now he won't budge. I quit. And, why didn't you get the toothpaste with stripes? I can't brush my teeth with this stuff.

Mother: Jimmy, you haven't eaten your breakfast yet. Brush your teeth afterward. How come that TV is on again? I'll go talk to Timmy, but Jim, I want you to tell him that was an accident. . . .

Morning (and bedtime) routines do not have to be accidents. In making books about family routines, we take the time to plan the do's and don'ts of what happens in our families every day. It can help us recognize our own rules for family living, and how the family members feel about living with those rules. Each of the examples that follow is designed for a different age group.

Timmy's Morning
(ages 2–6)

page 1: Morning is a busy time. Everybody has different jobs.
page 2: Timy has jobs, too. He is getting big.

page 3: He can put on his own undies, pants, socks and shirt. Mom and Dad help him pick out his clothes the night before.

page 4: After Timmy is dressed, he gets to pick what he wants for breakfast. He can pick from _____ or _____ or _____. When Mom or Dad has to help him get ready, there is less time, so Timmy can only have the cereal that Mom or Dad gives him.

page 5: When Timmy gets his jobs done he feels proud.
When Timmy is ready early, he can watch 15 minutes of one of his favorite shows on TV. Sometimes he makes a mistake and forgets, then he feels sad.

page 6: Mom and Dad can help Timmy to remember what his morning jobs are. Kate tells Timmy when she likes the colors he wears. Even Jimmy helps Timmy sometimes. Sometimes it's fun to have so many people in the family.

Kate Gets Off to School
(ages 6–11)

page 1: Our house is one of the busiest on the block. We have three kids and two grown-ups all going off in different directions. My little brother has to get ready for kindergarten, my big brother goes to junior high, and I'm in third grade. Both Mom and Dad work.

page 2: Mom usually helps us all out by making breakfast. Sometimes we have choices but when things get too rushed, we can only have cold cereal. Dad sometimes gives me a ride to the bus if I can be ready when he leaves the house at 7:45.

page 3: My job is to set the breakfast table, so I have to be downstairs before everybody else. If the table isn't set, it's harder for Mom to get things served.

page 4: Sometimes when I wake up late I feel grumpy about having to be the only one to have to take care of things for other people. Then I remember that Mom helps out in different ways, and so does Dad. Sometimes I wish I could trade jobs with Jimmy, and set the supper table instead.

page 5: My worst mornings are when I feel I've forgotten something for school, or when one of my girl-friends wants to go to school matching and there's nothing in my closet that has the colors in it that she told me on the telephone. I feel like yelling at Mom to get my pink shirt ready right now, even though I know she can't start ironing in the morning.

page 6: Sometimes it's really hard to live in such a busy house. Sometimes I wish I was an only child with servants instead of parents! But sometimes, when everything goes just right and I get a ride with Dad, we have a very special talk.

Adolescents have often outgrown the sort of books we have been discussing. But a written technique is still useful for spelling out the different pieces of the morning's demands, the adolescent's responsibilities, and the necessary family teamwork. Instead of a book, you can make some lists.

Jim's Morning Lists
(ages 12–16)

- Jim's list of what he thinks should happen in the morning
- Mom's and Dad's list of what Jim needs to get done
- Ways Mom and Dad can help
- What feels good and what feels bad about the routine

When we clarify the do's and don'ts of everyone's routines, we can also help each child to feel better at each step along the way. A successful completion of the morning (or evening) schedule can give children free time for what they want to do, or for a special reward in the form of additional choices. For each child, how Mom and Dad can (and can't) help is important. Children need us and need to feel we are on their side. The more parents can explain how kids can pitch in, and how the parents help out, the more we can all appreciate each other within the family.

As we saw, the book for children in the middle age range includes more complicated information than the book for younger children. For older children, sitting down to make a list together is usually the best way to proceed. Teenagers will feel more grown-up as participants. But whatever the age, each book or list should contain: 1) a description of the child's routine; 2) a description of common feelings the child has during the morning routine; and 3) a general, empathetic statement. Additional components could include a description of how parents can help and further incentives to keep the child on target.

In the following pages, we will see how to use stories in a number of ways that accentuate the positive aspects of new stages in life, such as how to support children in dealing with friendships at each point in their development.

HELPING WITH FRIENDS

Besides being used to help with home and school routines, homemade books can also be used to foster children's awareness of social relationships. The questions and confusions that children face in their friendships can be described in books, as well as the unique ways that children are naturally "good friends." Let's imagine we can overhear our preschooler playing with a friend. Our observations can be the starting point for a book to help a child feel proud of himself and his friendships.

Timmy: Let's make the road go over there. I can make a big mountain.

Freddy: I'll take my bulldozer and make a tunnel in your mountain. Oh-oh, it's caving in.

Timmy: We need more water. That mountain doesn't hold together. You start from that side and I'll start from this. Let's see if our hands can meet in the middle.

Freddy: I feel your hand.

Timmy: My Corvette is coming through. Make way! Look out! It's the fastest car here. I can make it do a pop-a-wheelie.

Freddy: My car is the fastest! It's going to zoom around the mountain. Let's make the road go over to here. Can we get enough water to make a lake? Do you have a boat we can use?

Timmy: My Mom says I can't put my boat in the sand. I can only use it in the bathtub.

Freddy: Look, I found a piece of bark. It can float. Let's see where it goes.

Timmy and Freddy Play Cars

A story could be written called "Timmy and Freddy Play Cars." Pages can be made to describe the situation. Examples: "Timmy and Freddy make a mountain." "Timmy and Freddy can make a tunnel when they help each other out." The next pages can describe some of the feelings: "It feels good to have fast cars." "It feels bad when your mountain begins to cave in." "Timmy was mad that Freddy's car went faster." The book can end with a general statement: "Sometimes when two friends can share an idea, they can have a lot of fun." "Sometimes when a plan is hard to do, friends have to talk it over." or "Sometimes, everybody likes to have the fastest car."

For a friendship between older children, a scrapbook format can be used to record special trips, to define ways that boys and girls sometimes have to share a best friend, or how different friends make different contributions—one may be more out-going, another may be easier to talk about personal matters, yet another may be most fun in activities, for example. In the dialogue that follows, a teenager is talking over a friendship problem with a parent.

Jim: Dad, you know that Buddy and Jeff never come over any more?

Father: I thought you guys just got together at the basketball court these days. I didn't know you wanted them to come over.

Jim: I still like video games, and we used to do them a lot, even after we had a game down on the court. But now, they just hang around by the corner store and wait for something to happen. It's kind of boring.

Father: So you're not sure you want to do that?

Jim: There's nothing to do there. Chad asks me to go over his house, but we always used to make fun of him. The last time I went with him, they made fun of me, too.

Father: So sometimes you feel left out and hurt when they tease you about a new friend?

Jim: Yeah. And you know what? They're smoking over there, too.

Father: Does that make you wonder about what you're supposed to do?

Jim: Sometimes I feel like a geek.

Father: It's tough to figure out where you belong when friendships start to change as you get older. Do you want to see if we can put down some ideas together about what you've noticed?

Jim: I guess so.

Jim's Buddies

- List of important friends
- Things they like and don't like
- What Jim likes and doesn't like
- General feelings about friendship

Once you have gotten into the habit of using books and lists to describe your child's experiences and feelings in an accepting way, problem solving is more easily shared. This foundation is needed even more as children move into adolescence. Teenagers are often tough to communicate with. They need their own space, but they also need our skills and greater experience to help them out with the new situations they have to face as young adults. Even though it may not hurt to hint now and then that you have an idea that may be of use to them, it is usually best to wait until you are invited.

< **3** >

Tools of the Trade

By now, the basic ideas of how to make books for children should have some shape in your mind. In this chapter, we will discuss ways to pull the story and the pictures together. Then we can explore how to encourage children to make their own books.

ARTWORK

Before I begin a story for—or in preparation for doing one with—a child, I always get set in my own mind how I want to describe the situation, how to recognize the child's feelings (and my own!), and what type of general statement I want to make, if any. If I jot my ideas down on a piece of paper, I can usually circle a few sentences that will go together on a page. Once I have made those decisions, I know how much blank space or how many facing pages there will be for illustrations.

Even if I have made the book in advance and done some of my own crude pictures, kids will often want to make new pictures or add new lines of their own. I welcome this as an opportunity to make the book bigger, richer, and even more a shared experience. Once we have the story together, we are ready to collect our materials for the art work, and to make the basic book.

TECHNIQUES

There are five basic techniques, all of which can be mixed and matched:

Drawing

1. Draw the pictures ourselves
2. Ask the child to draw them.
3. Do it together.

Scrapbook Methods

4. Cut and paste from magazines.
5. Use photographs.

Computers

6. Use to make borders.
7. Add in text.
8. Use a drawing or paint program to create images you and your child like.
9. Bring in cartoon art that can be stored in one of your programs.

The first books I made were with methods 1 to 5, before I had a computer. Some of the illustrations in this book, as you will see, are a combination of computer work and hand drawings.

To show some different ways we can use these techniques, we will describe books about three common school situations. The first, for the youngest child, deals with beginning school or daycare. The second involves something that we, as parents, teachers or counselors, should always attend to—commemorating special accomplishments—in order to support the development of a sound foundation of self-esteem. The third example shows how to use the listing technique with older children to help sort out their increasingly complex school schedules.

THINGS WE NEED

Tools and materials, at their simplest, are paper and magic markers, crayons, pens, or pencils. For the scrapbook technique, add old magazines, photos, and scissors. Pages can be held together with staples or paper fasteners, or with string tied through holes made with a punch or a pencil. Sometimes a book is only one page, glued or taped onto a larger piece of colored paper so it will last for a while. Remember, the important thing is how well you and your child work together. The artwork is just another way to deal with the topic and to increase the shared contact. Whether the drawings are by you or your child, acceptance and approval is the key. This is no time for comments like, "That horse looks like it needs a new head," or "You've gone out of the lines, Timmy."

Even the youngest children like to scribble, as a way of expressing ideas. We can support children's efforts by commenting on colors and designs in an approving way. This helps children to deal with the fact that their artwork does not always spring perfectly into view.

Sometimes children can have an attack of "perfectionitis" that can be daunting for parents. They may reject our drawings with comments like, "That doesn't look like our house, Mommy!" We are not all great artists, so we need to be prepared to say, perhaps with a sigh, "Well, you're very good at noticing things, but it reminds me of our house, and that was my idea. Do you want to make another house together? Or should we cut one out of a magazine? Maybe we can look for a photo of our house?"

Timmy's New School
techniques 1 and 2
artwork by parent, cover by child

page 1: I'm going to a new school.
page 2: It will have toys.
page 3: And kids to play with.
page 4: And teachers to help me.
page 5: And fun things to do.

In these introductory pages, special activities or interests of the child can be specified. If a child still needs help with the

I like my Teachers

I like my new friends

I like my new games

I like my new school.

potty, or at lunch time with certain foods, these facts can be built into the story or mentioned as the story is read to the child.

page 6: Mommy brings me to school.
page 7: Daddy picks me up.
pages 8 & 9: I give big hugs and kisses to say hello and to say goodbye.

The routines of separating from and rejoining the family are stated matter-of-factly. They are treated like learning to use a spoon. The routines and special features of the school day can also be described.

page 10: I have lunch at my school.
page 11: We take naps there, too.
page 12: We have snacks at our tables
page 13: where the floors are all blue.
page 14: Sometimes I miss Mom and Dad.
page 15: Sometimes I get mad at my friends.
page 16: Sometimes I don't like the school juice.
page 17: But teachers help me with words and hugs.

The child's negative feelings are accepted. Help from other adults is reaffirmed. It is understood that these unhappy moments are not the only ones the child will have.

page 18: I like my teachers.
page 19: I like my new friends.
page 20: I like my new games.
page 21: I like my new school.

The positive experiences of being at school are underlined.

Kate Wins a Spelling Star
techniques 3, 4 and 5
cover has photo of Kate holding her paper with a star

page 1: Kate has been working on her spelling lists all term. She studies them in her room. She makes a list.

Kate's Spelling Star

Kate has worked very hard. She has felt proud of her hard work. But she's been disappointed, too. She has never earned a spelling star. Usually one word has tripped her up. It's been hard to keep going without getting discouraged.

TOUGH WORDS

Here are all the hard words

1. _____   5. _____
2. _____   6. _____
3. _____   7. _____
4. _____   8. _____

Dad and Jim made a video about me!

KATE ACES SPELLING TEST

This week, Kate studied just as hard as ever. All of the words were tough. When she asked Dad how to spell one of them, he got it wrong! He couldn't believe it. He had to go look it up in the dictionary. Kate smiled to herself, but she knew that it's even hard for grown-ups to make mistakes.

LIST

MY STAR

This is the spelling list.

Mom even took us out for burgers as a treat the next day

Kate got every one right! She got her spelling star! She felt really proud. Mom and Dad and everyone at the supper table said "Congratulations!" to Kate.

It was tough to keep practicing. Kate knows that she may not get them all right next week, but she can feel really good about doing her best.

WHO KNOWS
WHAT I CAN
DO NEXT?

She asks Mom or Dad to practice the words with her before the test.

page 2: (picture from magazine of kid working at a desk, in school or at home)

page 3: Kate has worked very hard. She has felt proud of her hard work. But she's been disappointed, too. She has never earned a spelling star. Usually one word has tripped her up. It's been hard to keep going without getting discouraged.

page 4: (parent sets up page with list of difficult spelling words from past tests—ask child to highlight the toughest ones with a magic-marker)

page 5: This week, Kate studied just as hard as ever. All of the words were tough. When she asked Dad how to spell one of them, he got it wrong! He couldn't believe it. He had to go look it up in the dictionary. Kate smiled to herself, but she knew that it's even hard for grown-ups to make mistakes.

page 6: (Kate's drawing of Dad looking surprised)

page 7: This is the spelling list. (copy of her paper)

page 8: Kate got every one right! She got her spelling star! She felt really proud. Mom and Dad and every-one at the supper table said "Congratulations!" to Kate.

page 9: (picture from a magazine of a family at the dinner table)

page 10: It was tough to keep practicing. Kate knows that she may not get them all right next week, but she can feel really good about doing her best.

Books are wonderful testimonials. They should not be used only to identify difficult moments, but as a way to support and to celebrate all the positive things that children accomplish. We have to be sure that kids will not think, "Oh-oh, here comes trouble" every time they see a homemade book in our hands. And we have to remember that children can worry about any kind of "talking things over" until they feel reassured that our approach will accept their feelings, and see the situation from their point of view.

A book can also be used to identify, in a sympathetic way, frustrating aspects of school work. For teenagers, a list can clarify the routines of a new school semester. In making it together, we can discuss associated values and stress mutual goals to give our adolescents a broader perspective on most school situations, and, in the process, foster their sense of confidence and their ability to identify and manage their feelings. In this joint project, the parent took the initiative in finding the time to brainstorm together, getting the paper and pencil, and creating the topic headings.

Jim's Schedule at Junior High

SUBJECT	FEELINGS	GOALS FOR TERM	VALUE
Math	Hate it but easy	Pass	I can finish work

MAKING BOOKS WITH CHILDREN AND ENCOURAGING THEM TO MAKE BOOKS ON THEIR OWN

Let me begin this section with a story that resulted from a workshop on making books for children. One mother went straight home and applied her learning as soon as she walked in the door. Her little girl was trying very hard to be good about accepting the arrival of a baby brother, but the bad feelings were too strong for her. They were sneaking out in little pinches and hugs hard enough to make the baby cry. Her mother had tried talking to her about her anger, at both her new brother and her parents for making him, but the little girl steadfastly denied that she was mad about anything.

After our discussion group, the mother resolved to try again. She took a single piece of paper and divided it into boxes. At the top, she labeled one side "Things I Like about Babies" and the other "Things I Don't Like about Babies." After some hesitation, her daughter began making her lists. She liked it when her baby brother was happy, when they played together, and when they ate lollipops together. She didn't like it when he cried, when he bumped into a wall, and when he was sad. The artwork followed easily, and was even more fun. The little girl made pictures to fit into each box. She drew stick figures—one in a crib, two others in a box. She cheerfully announced that the figures were herself and the baby. Then, energized and relieved, she went on to practice making the letters of her name.

The same sort of interchange can be used when making a story together. You can sit beside your child with some paper and markers and say, "Let's make a story about your new school." Your child may launch into a fantastic tale, or convey some very disjointed ideas. Either is fine. Stick with it. Write down what is said and make the pictures together. Gradually more information, as well as the child's feelings, will emerge. Add a couple of pages from time to time during the week. Read the book over together at different times of the day. The project will get to be more and more fun.

If your child says, "I don't have any ideas," or "I don't know," try asking some simple questions: "What's your teacher like?" "What's fun about school?" "What don't you like?" Your book may be an odd assortment of pages, with lists alternating with seemingly unrelated pictures, but little by little an idea of your child's school will come together. The same approach can be used to help define ideas about your family, and anything else that affects your child.

The intensity of feelings within family life is the focus of our next chapter.

< **4** >

Stories About Feelings

As we have seen, two important skills that homemade books can help children develop are describing situations and feelings in their lives and forming general ideas about events. But when we begin to think about using these skills to make books about our own family life—our children's relationships to each other and to ourselves—we are often hesitant.

Writing books that give us all pats on the back for how we get along in the family may seem a little like bragging. But those of us who work with children have learned that a sense of pride, self-confidence, and self-esteem is necessary if children are going to function at their best. Not false pride, of course, or the "swelled-head syndrome," but a positive sense of themselves that comes from the ability to identify the positive moments that are part of everyone's experience. Just as we worked on identifying those moments in our child's school work and their friendships, we can also make books about positive times within the family.

Here's a typical situation that had a lot of danger points:

Jim: What are we having for dinner, Mom?

Kate: Don't tell me, I can smell it. Mom, you know I hate meatballs.

Jim: Too bad on you. Meatballs are my favorite.

Kate: I know, you *are* a meatball!

Mom: I know it's not your favorite, Kate, but *you* have to realize that everyone else in the family likes spaghetti and meatballs.

Timmy: Boing, boing, look at me bouncing!

Dad: Tim, That's pretty good. See if you can bounce over to the table with the napkins to help Kate set the table. Jim, the calendar says it's your week to clear the table and load the dishwasher.

Jim: I know, it's on my evening list.

Kate (from another room): Mom, do I *have* to eat that yucky stuff?

Mom: I know you wish you had something else, but tonight is spaghetti night.

Timmy (imitating): Yucky stuff, yucky stuff!

Dad: Tim, quiet down. It's time we all sat down.

Mom: Kate, bring in the salad while I bring the pasta. Dad is cutting the bread.

Timmy: Yucky stuff, yucky stuff!

Dad: Tim, supper time!

Timmy: Yucky spaghetti! I hate it! I don't want it!

Mom: Timmy, I don't like having my supper insulted. Kate, why did you get this started?

Kate (plaintively): Timmy, I have to eat it, too.

Timmy (starts to cry): I *can't* eat it. It makes my stomach hurt. Those meatballs all crowd up in my tummy!

Mom: Mmmmm...a crowded tummy? I hope it's not too crowded to make room for dessert after we finish our meal.

Kate: Timmy, I used to feel that way, too. Meatballs are still not my favorite. You know why? I used to think those meatballs would just bounce around in my tummy, and Mom and Dad would have to bounce me to bed.

Timmy (sniffling, but crying less): Daddy, would you bounce me?

Jim: I bet Dad'll bounce you good after he helps me with my math. (Timmy cries harder.)

Dad (sternly): Jim!

Jim: Well, maybe we could switch, and have Dad bounce you first. Besides, Timmy, you know you like my muscles. Where do you think they come from? Let me show you. Don't you see a meatball in there?

(Timmy starts to laugh a little.)

Mom: Well, let's just get started with this meal.

Dad: Agreed.

Kate and Jimmy Help Out
or
The Meatball Escapade

page 1: Supper time is a busy time for everybody, but we all get together and try to share some time. Mom gets everything going, and when Dad comes home from work he pitches in, too. Kate, Timmy, and Jim all have suppertime jobs.

page 2: Sometimes we eat things everybody likes, sometimes we don't. We all eat the same meal, so sometimes some people are happier than others. One night it was meatball night.

page 3: Jim said: Meat balls—Neat-O!
Kate said: Meatballs—Oh No!
Timmy said: Meatballs—YUCK-O!

page 4: Timmy started to cry because he thought meatballs would bunch up in his tummy.

page 5: But Kate said: Meatballs give you bounce!
And Jim said: Meatballs give you muscles!

page 6: Mom and Dad said: Let's have supper. Everyone doesn't get to eat their favorite meal every night, but some nights they do.

Family interactions tap into basic human emotions. There are five kinds of feelings that all children need to learn how to identify: *glad, sad, mad, scared,* and *"bad."* Making them rhyme is one way to be sure they are easy to recall. By the age of two, most children can label times when they are glad, mad, sad and scared. By three or four, these feelings are usually clearer and associated with a variety of events, and the child is often ready to understand what a "bad" feeling is. Children can deal with their emotions better when parents help identify them in a nonjudgmental way.

Glad, of course, identifies happy feelings. *Sad, mad,* and *scared* are pretty straightforward; most parents and children can readily identify these states. Throughout childhood, most situations that make children sad can also make them mad. It is important to try to help children understand this, since using anger to protect oneself from sadness or hurt continues, for many people, to be a complication in adult life.

Scared feelings may also lurk in the background of nearly every emotional situation. Children, like adults, are often concerned that, whatever their feelings, they may get out of control, and this is frightening.

"Bad" is a generic term that can refer to feeling guilty, or to being in a "low" or "blue" mood. Once a child comes to terms with these basic feelings, recognition of shadings and blendings will evolve, just as children's recognition eventually extends from primary colors to subtle combinations of tones.

In the course of normal family living, unpleasant emotions may often be aroused: anger, disappointment, confusion, and jealousy, to name only a few. These feelings can be as difficult to talk about as body parts or the "facts of life," so parents tend to hope that whatever aroused them will quietly disappear. But we all know better. After all, our own negative feelings don't just slink away—we have to deal with them, one way or another. One of the best ways to manage them is also the simplest: to talk about them.

Talking about negative feelings can be scary. But talking with (and, especially, listening to) our children about them leads to an increased sense of confidence and to trust in the bonds of the family unit. Talking out negative feelings keeps them from being stored up, from becoming grudges or a chip on the shoulder, and from getting acted out in troublesome ways.

Often, in families, the most difficult interactions touch upon anger. It is important that anger be understood, clearly labeled, and worked on throughout most relationships. Nowhere is this more true than in the midst of life with children, where the cauldron of emotion can boil over so easily. Let us look at another family exchange:

Mom: Kids, Dad's running a little behind schedule, so supper's going to be a little late.

Jim: Does that mean he won't have time to go over my math?

Kate: Or that I won't get to watch the beginning of my favorite show?

Mom: Kate, we can talk that over in a minute. Jim, I'd like to ask you to discuss how Dad feels and what he *can* do tonight *after* supper, alright? Do you get the picture?

Jim: Yeah, Mom.

Kate: So when *will* we eat?

Mom: Probably by seven.

Kate (sarcastically): Great!

Mom: I know how you feel, but your Dad didn't plan for this to happen, you know. Oh, I think I hear him now.

Timmy: Daddy, Daddy!

Dad: Okay, okay, big boy! Get yourself to the table. Kate, how come the table isn't set?

Kate: We thought you were going to be later and . . .

Dad (clearly in a bad mood): No excuses, just get it done.

Mom: Was work that bad?

Dad (not wanting any discussion): No.

Mom: Kids, let's get to the table.

Jim: Dad?

Mom: Jim, hold off for a bit and go get some butter from the kitchen.

Kate: You know, Sally wore a new stonewashed denim miniskirt to school and everybody really loved it. I'd like to have something new to wear to the party for the school play. So when we get to go shopping again. . .

Timmy: I want to come! I need a new coloring book.

Dad: Please pass the bread.

Timmy: My last coloring book got all messed up when Jenny came over and did all the pictures with Cinderella and she didn't leave any for me and. . .

Kate: Timmy, you can't color Cinderella, anyway. You gave her black hair in all the pictures you did.

Timmy: MOMM-MY!

Mom: Kate, if you want me to finish working on your projects like the play and be thinking about another shopping trip, I'd like some cooperation. I remember when you told Timmy he was one of your favorite colorers, in his Dumbo book.

Dad (sounding frustrated): Please, pass the bread.

Jim: Here's the butter, and, Mom, did you wash my sweatpants? I wanted them after basketball practice and couldn't find them.

Kate: Mom, you still haven't answered me.

Dad (thumps the table): Pass the bread, dammit!
(Timmy starts to cry.)

Kate (anxious): Here, here it is, Dad. I'm sorry, I'm really sorry. I didn't notice it was next to me.

Jim (muttering): Sheesh! If I ever did that, I'd be sent to my room before dinner was even over.

Mom: Kate, it's alright, your Dad has the bread now.

Timmy (scared and crying): Is Daddy mad? Does he hate us?

Mom: Timmy, it's okay. Lou, look what you started.

Dad (stern): Doesn't ANYONE listen in this family?

Kate (nervously): I do, Dad, I mean, I tried, but I guess I didn't. Dad, can I get you anything else?

Mom: That's fine, Kate. Let's just make sure that everything's on the table, and then we'll see if we can get started again.

No matter how difficult it is to acknowledge difficult moments, mistakes, problems with temper, or any other negative emotions, we must be able to be honest enough to admit that such things do indeed occur. Even trained professionals encounter these problems in their own families! The best we can do is to identify them quickly and clearly, to make sure we talk them through, and to try a little harder next time.

How many times have I told myself that I would greet my children's work with words of praise and instead found myself saying "If you'd listened to my advice, it would've been a lot better"? How many times have I had to swallow my pride and go back and review the situation with my child so that we could both feel comfortable with our relationship?

Children do not feel good about themselves when their efforts (best or otherwise) are greeted by moralizing, sarcasm, lectures, warnings, or statements of disappointment. They need to be helped to evaluate what they have done in such a way that their appraisals can be acted upon, and their own problem-solving abilities engaged. Similarly, we do not feel good about ourselves when we have acted in ways that do not measure up to our own expectations of ourselves as parents.

These things happen, though, no matter who we are. How many times have I lost my temper when a chore has not been completed or a troublesome event has come up? I've had to swallow my words—but first I've had to grit my teeth and admit that I said them. Making room for bad feelings *does* make room for good ones. And creating books about those worst moments allows for some honest sharing about what happened and what was felt, and what could be changed to deal with them better in the future.

Pass the Bread, Dammit!

page 1: Some nights our family is just too busy. Everybody needs something different. Jim needs help with his math, Kate wants to think about a shopping trip, and Timmy needs some special attention, too. Mom has had to get everything ready for Kate's play rehearsal, and Dad's boss has asked him to stay late. What a day!

page 2: It was a big rush to get everything ready and on the table for supper. Everybody wanted a turn to speak.

page 3: Daddy was really tired and easily frustrated. He said Pass the bread, but no one heard. Finally, *Bang!* he thumped the table, and everyone got scared.

page 4: Timmy cried and was scared about Daddy's mad feelings. Kate worried about not doing the right thing. Jim grouched about Dad's bad mood.

page 5: Everybody needed some extra time, but first we all had to finish our supper and talk over our plans for the evening.

page 6: Sometimes it's hard when everyone feels frustrated.

Negative feelings do not occur only at times of family frustration. Younger children may need help in dealing with nighttime fears, or problems to do with sports, or friendships that make them feel angry or left out. Adolescents may face increased pressures from competition, sexuality, and new responsibilities. With each of these, either the book format or the listing technique can lead to creative exchanges.

The story will be right if whatever is the matter is described in an accepting way. The book may simply tell about how a child is feeling; explaining the actual cause of the distress is not necessary.

For instance, a three-year-old has been having trouble separating from her mother. The story can be:

Jody's Story

page 1: Jody had a nightmare again last night. Mommy had to go in to give her an extra kiss. Daddy gave her a hug the night before when she cried.

page 2: Sometimes when she goes to her babysitter, she cries

too. She doesn't like to say goodbye to Mommy or
Daddy.

page 3: At supper time, she only wants Mommy to help her.
Sometimes Mommy says, "Jody, you need to let
Daddy help you, too." Jody doesn't like that.

After reading this story together with her parents a few
times, Jody may share some additional information or may
just become more relaxed because her parents have let her
know that her "hard time" has been noticed.

Everyone is better off when they know what they are feeling,
when they are feeling it. Making books about feelings helps
children know that they do not have to be scared of their
feelings. It also helps us, as their parents, to remember that
we do not have to be, either. Helping our children manage their
feelings as they occur gives them good equipment for
managing life on their own later on. When a family gets into
the habit of identifying and accepting their feelings, they have
not only affirmed the bond between them, they have also
enhanced their sense of companionship. They all feel understood. They are calmer and can better understand each other's
point of view.

An important thing to remember, though, is that, in most
situations, *there can be more than one feeling, and they can be
contradictory!* But once a book is created that acknowledges
their existence, children can come to realize that neither the
feelings nor the situations are going to last forever.

‹ 5 ›

Longer Stories

The books we have considered so far are short depictions of a situation or feeling. They do not have true storylines or plots with beginnings, middles, and ends. But sometimes we will want to write longer stories for our children in order to clarify a reality, prepare them for a change, or review some of life's experiences. "A New Baby for the Family" was written to prepare my daughter, Lisa, for the birth of her brother, Jeffrey. It can serve as an illustration for our discussion of how to construct longer stories.

BEGINNINGS

In "Alice in Wonderland," when Alice asks the Red Queen how to tell her tale, she receives very good advice: Begin at the beginning. This is what you have to do in making a book for your child. The beginning should carry you, the reader, straight into the story; it should engage your curiosity, or sense of fun. Engaging children's attention with the content of any book is very important, if you want them to listen and to learn.

Engagement is prompted by a spirit of acceptance and playfulness. Stories should start with whatever the situation is, and should accept it with a positive spirit. This acceptance is an essential step in getting the child involved with the story. A variety of devices will capture children's attention. Two of them—the use of repetition and the use of the child's name—are familiar features in the play repertoire of most preschoolers.

However your story begins, it is important for it to "tell it like it is." It may be that a child may not like the event you are about to describe, or, as in "A New Baby for the Family," that the changes associated with it prompt some pain or aggravation. Negative feelings or other anticipated reactions of the child need to be identified by the parents when first thinking about the storyline. The background elements should show that these reactions are accepted and understood. Only then can the story get underway.

Two sorts of beginnings particularly appeal to children. One picks a significant starting point and marches the story onward from there toward the final event. The other way to get going is to state a theme. Both beginnings can capture a child's attention. "A New Baby for the Family" uses the second approach. The theme is established using numbers to represent the difference between now and what is to come. The change this little girl faces is that her family will increase in size from four to five members.

If you use a theme, it should be defined and repeated in a variety of ways. The end should resolve or refer back to the initial theme.

The following book was the first long one I made for my daughter, Lisa. You can see from the illustration that the art work did not depend on any artistry, just finding an image for the ideas. Held together by string, it nonetheless delighted Lisa and helped her a lot.

A New Baby for the Family

page 1: This story was written by a little girl – ME! 1

page 2: Here is my family: Mommy, Daddy, Lisa, Toby – 1, 2, 3, 4

page 3: Oops! Count again! 1 Daddy, 2 Lisa, 3 Toby,

page 4: 4 Mommy, 5 Baby

page 5: Look, Daddy, look how big Mommy's tummy is.

My School

Tot Lot

I am big enough to go to school. I have lots of friends.

Goo Goo

My friends know that my Mommy is going to have a baby. We play Mommy, Daddy and baby together.
I like to play baby and cry and say goo goo.

But I also like to play Mommy and pretend to carry the baby. I also like to be a little girl and play games with my friends.

Daddy goes with me to the restaurant. We have tea together. I don't cry or fuss.
I am a big girl.

Daddy carries me upstairs to bed at night now. Then Mommy tucks me in.

Blankie   fuzzy

Teddy

One day my Mommy says oh, oh, my tummy hurts. The Baby is coming!

So Mommy goes to the hospital with Daddy so the baby can come out.

My big friends Sara and Sally come to stay with me and we have a little party together.

party cake

A Surprise! My Grammy comes to visit.

She is lots of fun and she is going to stay with us for awhile.

Candy

Daddy brings me home a candy from the hospital where Mommy is staying. I like it

Mommy comes home
with The new baby.

I give The new
baby a Kiss.

The baby is
a little boy. He
looks very funny and
tiny. I am so much
bigger. I am a little
girl with a brother.

Me

Jeffrey

It is funny
to wait for a new
baby

1.   2.

3   4   5

It is funny to have a
New baby at home too.

page 6: Mommy's tummy is getting bigger and bigger
page 7: and BIGGER.
page 8: Soon springtime will be here and the baby will be ready to come out.

Identifying the change in noticeable ways (like Mommy's size) and helping the child with a sense of time (spring) are two ways the story helps the child prepare.

page 9: Here is Mommy taking a nap. She gets tired and sleepy these days.
page 10: Sometimes she gets mad, too!
page 11: She can't go up and down stairs so easily anymore.
page 12: Sometimes she gets very quiet and dreams about what things will be like with the new baby.

The child will appreciate knowing that new events influence the thoughts, feelings, and behavior of others, too!

page 13: My School. I am big enough to go to school.
page 14: I have lots of friends.
page 15: My friends know my Mommy is going to have a baby. We play mommy, daddy, and baby together.
page 16: I like to play baby and cry and say, "Goo-goo."
page 17: I like to play mommy and pretend to carry the baby.
page 18: I also like to be a little girl and play games with my friends.

The child is identified as BIG. No matter what age she is, she will be bigger than the new baby. The child's ability to master new events through play is accepted. The child is also accepted as being able to be both big (as school) and little (still needing contact and comfort).

page 19: Daddy goes with me to the restaurant.
page 20: We have dinner together. I don't fuss or cry. I am a big girl.

page 21: Daddy carries me upstairs to bed at night now. Mommy tucks me in.

page 22: (blankie, fuzzy, teddy bear pictures)

The role of other people is accentuated: father, friends, grandparents, or neighbors. The child will be pleased to be reminded that there are other helpers when Mommy does not feel well or will have new jobs to do.

page 23: One day Mommy says, "Oh-oh. My tummy hurts. The baby is coming."

page 24: Daddy drives Mommy to the hospital so the baby can come out.

page 25: My big friends Sara and Sally come to stay with me.

page 26: We have a little party together.

The child is reassured that she is not forgotten. No matter how busy it gets, her needs will be met, and there will still be time for something special.

page 27: A surprise! Grammy comes to visit.

page 28: She is lots of fun, and she is going to stay with us for a while.

page 29: Daddy brings me home candy from the hospital where Mommy is staying.

page 30: I like it. He brings my favorite kind.

page 31: Mommy comes home with the new baby.

page 32: I give the baby a kiss.

page 33: The baby is a boy. He looks funny and tiny.

page 34: I am much bigger. I am a big sister with a little brother.

Positive acceptance is stressed, and the little girl's new sense of herself as a big sister is underlined.

page 35: It is funny to wait for a new baby.

page 36: It is funny to have a new baby at home, too.

The last two pictures show Toby, Jeffrey, Lisa, Mommy, and Daddy, with numbers 1, 2, 3, 4, 5. The numbers remind the child of the beginning of the story and of the new family size. The term "funny" is used to allow and encourage conversation about the child's new feelings about the baby.

Here is an alternate way that "A New Baby for the Family" could begin, for another child:

page 1: Michael didn't like changes.

page 2: When the sun came up in the morning, Michael would say, "I don't want to get up."

page 3: When the dark gathered around the house in the evening, Michael would say, "I don't want to go to bed."

page 4: When there wasn't peanut butter and jelly for lunch, Michael would say, "I don't want any lunch."

page 5: Michael didn't like changes.

page 6: Michael liked his family just the way it was now. He didn't want a new baby.

page 7: Now, there are four people in his family. . . .

The theme, in this case, is a dislike of change. Most children do not like changes, as any preschooler could tell you. This story helps the child to understand that point by repeating it in various forms. Repetition also helps to establish a rhythm for the story. The child's name can be used over and over, as can an idea. Use as many different concrete examples as you can think of to allow the child to catch onto the concept.

The objective of engaging the child's attention will be defeated if you begin the story with a moral (a concept with a value judgment attached) or with how you want your child to behave or feel. While you naturally want to help Michael to be happier with the changes in the family, unless the story begins by comfortably stating that Michael *doesn't* like them, you will only alienate him. Simply spell out his feelings, and proceed from there. This step, paradoxically, can make it easier for your child to come around to a new point of view. The beginning of your child's book should not be a reintroduction of a familiar struggle, or another lecture. If it is, the beginning will quickly become the end; the child will simply tune out.

Since life is such a jumble of events, finding a good beginning may be difficult. So be arbitrary—just pick one. The story about the arrival of a new baby, for yet another example, could start with two sets of grandparents and two old babies (Mom and Dad) and how they arrived in their families. Another page could have them meet and marry. The next could describe the addition of the first new baby (the child the story is being read to), in preparation for the counting page. If the child has a long enough attention span, and a good connection to the grandparents, this type of beginning can help her think about becoming a part of the larger human community. The ideas of sharing, helping, and mutual dependence can be reviewed. In this way, the beginning of your story can also be the beginning of another whole set of ideas.

Alternatively, if your child is old enough and you want to introduce some simple sexual information, the story could begin with Stanley Sperm and Elsa Egg. The brief inclusion of some scientific facts, like sperm and egg uniting, can help the child relate to other books on this topic. It can serve as a reminder that some books are not just for amusement, but have to do with real-life happenings.

Beginnings can use other devices, such as introducing a favorite topic or interest. "A New Baby for the Family" uses counting, a preschool talent that can often focus a child's interest. The beginning does not need to rely only on the story itself or on the pictures, but instead on one of the child's emerging skills. Obviously, each child is unique, with special interests and favorite things or activities. For a child who is especially interested in colors, the beginning could be modified this way:

page 1: Here is my family. 1, 2, 3, 4.
page 2: Daddy is wearing dark green.
page 3: Mommy is dressed in yellow.
page 4: I'm wearing my favorite color: purple.

page 5: My dog has a red collar on.
page 6: OOPS, count again, 1, 2, 3, 4, 5! We have a new baby.
          I wonder what color he will like?
page 7: Mommy and Daddy and I will pick some colors for
          him. For his blanket, for his room and for some of
          his clothes. . . .

A good beginning involves the child with the idea of the
new event or the nature of the problem. But once the theme
has been stated and the devices set in motion, we are ready to
move on.

THE MIDDLE

The middle of the story contains the message(s). In "A
New Baby for the Family," there are three key messages:
1) Mommy is different now, and that is okay. 2) Daddy has
a new place in the child's care (another way of saying that
the child's needs will still be met). 3) The child is getting
bigger.

Each message pertains to the impending change. Each
confirms the child's experience, but also contains a little bit of
"brain-washing." Each of the messages helps a child to "frame,"
or develop a point of view about what is happening: Change
can be okay. It means that even though Mom is different now,
or Dad does more helping out around the house, or the child
is growing up, it is going to be alright—in fact, the child may
even be pleased with the new situation! These messages make
explicit much of the teaching that parents try to do all the
time, but on a less conscious level.

The tone of the first message—that Mommy is different
now—is one of sympathetic acceptance: "This is how it is. And
it's okay." One way that Mommy is different is that her tummy
is bigger, but that is not all. She is tired more often, perhaps
even grouchy, and less able to be attentive to every little thing.
She has less strength and energy (she does not carry the child
up to bed anymore).

The second message underscores how Daddy is beginning to take over more of the child's caretaking. He does the carrying to bed now; he thinks of special treats. This message provides the reassurance all children need, especially during change. It says: Even if Mommy is busy, there will be someone to take care of you, to nurture you and meet your needs. Someone will be there, thinking about you, even if there is a lot of hurry and scurry because of the new baby.

It does not, of course, have to be Daddy—a grandparent, a close friend, or anyone intimately involved in the family's life will do. In Lisa's story, Sara and Sally were important adults in her life. They can help her now, just as they did before. Even with new babies around, there will still be time and attention for the older child.

One difference a new baby makes is that the older child needs to put up with less, one way or another—less attention, less time, less closeness. But it also means gaining something. That is message number three: The child's status as bigger and more competent is confirmed. T-shirts proclaiming "I'm a Big Brother" or "I'm a Big Sister" have popularized this concept. Even a child with extremely weak skills, or one who is only a year older than the baby, can do much more than a newborn. These comparative strengths should be emphasized in positive ways. (But remember to avoid those "Cut that out— you're too big!" messages. Children experiencing the addition of a new baby to the family still need a place where they can be "little.") The older child can pitch in. Instead of always needing help, the child can now be a helper with the new sibling sometimes. The story can point out various ways this might occur.

Each message is defined as part of what is happening. The changes are nobody's fault. The story suggests that no one can really expect things in the family to be otherwise. Each change (Mommy's new state, Daddy's new roles, and the child getting bigger) is a harbinger of other changes. With a new baby in the house, things will indeed be different.

These messages reflect things that you may feel your child "knows," but is not able to put into words yet. Concrete examples and known reference points (like blankies and teddies) will help the child relate to and understand the messages. The language should be pared down and the ideas stated as simply as possible.

Defining what the messages should be requires some thought, and the vision of an adult who can see more than one side of life's dilemmas. It is not always easy to do. In many situations, there may be pain, loss, or anger, but there is also, always, an opportunity for growth. Children need to be helped to understand, accept, and cope with any troublesome feelings along the way.

There are times when we, as parents, cannot see clearly how to define what the message should be, or where to find the hope and experience needed for a resolution to the problem. At these times the guidance of someone with expertise in child development and family life may be necessary. Once you understand and can cope with the larger picture in your own terms, you should have less trouble in translating that understanding into a book for your child.

Storybooks are an important part of a child's introduction to life events. Play is another way that children have of coping with new events, and it can be encouraged in your story. In "A New Baby for the Family," for example, there is the suggestion that Lisa try playing out "being baby" or "being mommy" with her dolls or friends. Sometimes the child's less acceptable feelings are expressed in this sort of play, which can help the child to manage anger—even when it takes the form of putting the baby in the toilet or the oven!

For a child struggling with troublesome feelings, the story might show a child who is preoccupied with them. She could, for instance, stamp her feet and demand that Mommy carry her upstairs, or she could cry bitterly when the baby's crib is painted. Then, little by little, the story could describe how such feelings come to be accepted. These special bedtime stories, play, and the little talks that parents have with children can all contribute to a child's readiness for what comes next: the ending.

ENDINGS

While the ending presents the "main event," it can, none-theless, be a minor part of a homemade storybook. In "A New Baby for the Family," the facts about the impending birth are clarified, but the child's associated concerns have already been addressed. The book has put the birth in the context of the normal flow of events, and reassured the child that life will go on in a comfortable way.

In "A New Baby for the Family," the fact that the ending is not quite "the end" is also suggested. "It's funny to wait for a new baby. It's funny to have a new baby in the house, too." The word "funny" is used here because it is ambiguous. It leaves room to ask children what they think things might be like. It suggests that the new baby coming may have aroused some discomfort, and that having the new baby around might, too. Now these things can be discussed, and new questions can lead to additional pages or to another book. The ground has already been prepared for the sequel: "There's a New Baby in Our House!"

Once you have written one longer storybook, and shared the delight of reading it together and talking about it, making others becomes easier and easier. The more aware you are of normal feelings and reactions, the less you will worry about putting ideas or feelings into your child's mouth. At the same time, it is important to be sure that your own worries and fears do not creep into the story. All parents tend to worry about disappointing or upsetting their children, and we often have to work at keeping guilt and confusion at bay. This issue will be discussed further in Chapters 6 and 7, in dealing with situations where change or loss can make a parent more vulnerable.

Lisa's storybook presented her with a "worst case" scenario (a baby brother instead of the sister she was hoping for) to help her adjust to the fact that this new baby might not be exactly what she wanted. The concept that you can't always get (or give) what you want is, of course, one that has to be dealt with throughout childhood, and adult life as well. All too often, this bitter truth is communicated by parents in an angry way, when they are frustrated by the child's recurrent demands or persistent dissatisfaction. But adding anger to it alters the message by incorporating blame. The child continues to experience frustration as either her own fault or her parents' fault. This can lead to a chip-on-the-shoulder, negative attitude. Patience is best nurtured by a sympathetic acceptance of the dismay that accompanies not getting what you want, even while you help your child to understand that you will continue to do your best to provide whatever she needs.

The love of children for their very *own* stories was brought home to me by my daughter and son, Lisa and Jeffrey, and by the many children whose parents asked me to help fashion books for them. At first, I made stories that merely resembled the family I was helping, altering details. I believed that a story that was close, but not exactly like their own, might be more interesting, and that a child might be less embarrassed than if her own life was right there on the page. But when those books were read, the children would always correct every detail, saying, "No, no, that's wrong!" and proceed to make all names and events line up with what they knew to be true. So, as I listened to their reactions, I began to trace their lives and their feelings more accurately in my stories. The children had an unflinching interest in the stories being *right,* no matter how difficult or traumatic the contents.

LIFE REVIEWS

One of the nicest uses I have found for longer books for children is as a way of looking back over a period of time and remembering the good moments, as well as some of the bad. This has been especially valuable at the end of a school year, when teachers can help children remember their challenges and their achievements. It helps to bring a sense of definition to the child's positive feelings about what has been achieved, and also acknowledges that some of that growing up was not easy.

Children love to be reminded of their "getting bigger." It makes them aware of the time it takes to grow, not just in size, but in behavior and knowledge. Children can enjoy this sense of pride with books show their past activities and mastery of skills. Everyone can feel good after putting together one of these books. For the older child, parent-guided (or simply encouraged) scrapbooks are helpful, while a "life review list" can be satisfying for an adolescent.

Anthony's Goodbye Book
(a book for a younger child)

page 1: One day, a new boy came to school. His name was Anthony. His teacher said, "Hello, Anthony. Welcome to our school." All the kids said "hello," too.

page 2: Anthony met his special helper at school. His name was Greg. Greg helped Anthony and other boys to learn new things and to figure out how to be good friends.

page 3: Anthony learned all about his school. He learned about choice time and circle time. He learned about snack time and table time and his favorite time of all: outside time! Greg helped Anthony remember the rules at school so that he could have fun and be safe.

page 4: When table time came, all the kids had to work on special projects. Some kids were working on letters, others were working on numbers. Greg learned all about the activities Anthony liked to do

page 5: and what he *didn't* always like to do. Greg helped Anthony learn to do those things, too—even if sometimes they made Anthony mad and he said, "I don't want to practice my letters. I hate it!"

page 6: All the teachers worked together to help kids share and take turns. When Anthony wanted a turn on the swing, Greg helped him to get one by asking, and waiting. Sometimes teachers had to use timers to help kids take turns. The timer was another helper.

page 7: One day, Greg told Anthony that he was going to have to say goodbye. He showed Anthony the day he would leave on the calendar. Together they made a special calendar so that they could count the days together.

page 8: When there were only four more days left, Greg gave Anthony a special book. It was a goodbye book that Greg had made. They read it together.

page 9: Greg cannot come to school anymore. He moved away and has a new job. He thinks about Anthony and all the special things they did together. Greg misses Anthony and all the other boys and the teachers at school.

page 10: Anthony still comes to school. He has fun and learns new things at school. Whenever Anthony thinks about Greg, his special friend, he reads this goodbye book. It has a place on the shelf, just as Anthony has a place in Greg's heart.

Kate's Scrapbook of (year)
(for the older children)

Challenges of (year)
(for the adolescent)

	CHALLENGES TO DATE	CHALLENGES TO COME
School		
Friends		
Activities		
Sports		
Travel		
Family		
Special Events		

LIFE REVIEWS FOR CHILDREN IN SPECIAL SITUATIONS

Some children need books that look back over time to help them make some sense of their lives and the different situations they have had to face because their parents, for one reason or another, have been unable to care for them. These children may have had to endure periods of neglect, moving from one foster-care arrangement to another. At the point when a book is made, they may finally be in a more permanent home, with an adoptive family or a grandparent. They need the reassurance that they will be cared for in a better way from now on, and also, on some very elementary level, that they were wanted and loved as babies by their biological parents.

Many foster parents and grandparents are reluctant to let these children hear about their own lives, fearing the experience might further traumatize them. Whenever I have made such books, though, the kids have shown a sense of relief as they see a recognition and validation of what they have experienced, and as they are helped to draw neutral conclusions. Here is a brief example:

Jeanette's Story

page 1: Jeanette lives with her grandmother, Ma, and her Grandpa Al. She has uncles and aunts who live with her, too. Her Mom is the sister of Uncle Bill, Uncle Sal, Aunt Jeannie, and Aunt Liz.

page 2: Jeanette's Mom doesn't live with her or the family. When her Mom was 17, Jeanette was born in a city far from home. Jeanette's Mom said, "I love this baby." But, day by day, it was hard for her Mom to take care of Jeanette. She said, "I need some help."

page 3: Different people in the city tried to help. First there was a family that tried to help, but that didn't work. Then there was a home for kids where

Jeanette lived for two years. She had some grown-up helpers that she liked. She liked some of the other kids, too.

page 4: Then Ma came. She said, "I'm your Grandma and I'm going to take you home with me. Your Mom is still sick and can't take care of you. We will be your family."

page 5: Sometimes Jeanette feels sad about not having a Mom like the other kids at school. She wonders about her Mom and wishes she'd get better and come back. Jeanette asks Ma about it. They talk together.

page 6: Sometimes Jeanette worries about losing her home again, but Ma says, "You're home now and this is where you will be."

A story like this can have many variations. Some children have more specific memories of places, people, and even traumatic events that they want included. There may be more information about a parent's illness that can be introduced. For some, it helps to explain that a particular vulnerability to drugs or alcohol exists within their family (this may be an important foundation for their own caution in the future). Children need to struggle with the concept that even though adults may have wished to be caring and protective, they were unable to make good choices, just as children sometimes forget to do the right thing. Information about their lives can, in the long run, help these children put those events behind them, and can lead to the fresh starts they need to make.

All of the endings in these stories can lead to new beginnings. Our books can beget second editions when our first editions are both honest and accepting. One of the great pleasures of having children is being able to share in the wonder and new feelings that accompany each new "page" in their lives. The next chapter helps parents think further about helping a child through new developmental steps or major family transitions. Storybooks can help children focus on the preparations they must make for a change, and can lead to a sense of being able to manage it more easily.

< 6 >

Stories About Growing Up

Stories can be written to help a child take a step forward while growing up. For some children, this may mean developing a better sense of self-control, for others, the sadness of putting away their teddy bear as their best friend. Of course, growing up is a mixed blessing. Let us look at a possible discussion between a parent and a child on the joys of learning to use the toilet by yourself:

Mother: Timmy, you look like you need to go to the bathroom.

Timmy: No. No, I don't.

Mother: How come you have the wiggles, then? That looks like your pee-pee dance to me.

Timmy: No, Mommy.

Mother: Timmy, remember, I'm trying to help you. You know, if you wait until the last minute, you can get yourself all wet.

Timmy: Mommy, why won't you play cars with me?

Mother: Timmy, it's not time for playing, it's time for talking. . . .Timmy, come out from under the table.

Timmy: Choo, choo, the train is coming through! *(he hears someone flushing the toilet, then suddenly shrieking)* Oh-oh! Mommy, Mommy! I have to pee!

Mother: Timmy, what did I just tell you? You're not acting like
    a big boy at all.

Timmy: I don't *want* to be a big boy!

What answer do we have for that one? Well, it might be one
that could be found in a homemade book for Timmy called "I
Don't Want to Be Big." The abilities we have gained by now,
for describing situations, behaviors, and feelings nonjudg-
mentally, and then making a general and empathic statement
about them, can come in handy.

Is it so surprising, after all, that a child might resist one
more task of "being big"? As preschoolers, children have to
manage more new developmental steps, in a shorter period
of time, than they will at any other time in their entire lives.
Growing older and getting bigger is always more than a
little scary. Inevitably it means giving some things up, as
well as gaining others. Loss and change result in sad feelings even when there are exciting adventures ahead. Like
adults, children can have more than one feeling about any
life experience.

Hopefully, we can help our children deal with the necessary
losses, help them feel a little less afraid of taking necessary
steps, and, when they do, help them achieve a new sense of
mastery and pride in their accomplishment, so they can
conclude that this step forward, at least, was worth the
trouble, after all.

But moving forward should never mean losing one's sense
of security. Just as when toddlers are beginning to take those
first steps in their journeys away from us, they still need to be
able to turn around and see that their cheering section is right
there behind them and ready, in case they feel a little shaky,
to keep them from falling. Those old sources of reassurance
(whether a blankie, a bottle, or a favorite comic) should never
be put completely out of reach. Everyone needs some sort of
security blanket.

Now let us look at the book we made for Timmy called "I
Don't Want to Be a Big Boy":

I Don't Want to Be a Big Boy

page 1: I really like to play. I like to play with my cars and trains. I like to play with my trucks. I like to play with my friend Ben.

page 2: I go to the store with Mommy, and I go to nursery school, too. Sometimes I get so busy I forget to go pee-pee, and then I get wet.

page 3: Mommy says: Is that your pee-pee dance?
Mommy says: Do you need to go to the bathroom?
Mommy says: Timmy, go to the bathroom right now.

page 4: Sometimes I just want to play.
Sometimes I don't notice my pee-pee dance.
Sometimes I get mad and sad when I'm wet and I say: I don't want to be a big boy.

page 5: I like to be a big boy when I go to the store. I like to be a big boy when I can play with Ben outside all by myself. I'm big enough to catch a ball, too.

page 6: Sometimes when Mommy says, Pick up your toys, I wish I didn't have to be big. It's a hard job.

page 7: Sometimes it's hard to be a big boy all the time.

Some children need to learn how to use words instead of expressing their anger through tantrums. Others could use help in managing a new family bedtime routine. Because these two problems are so common among preschoolers, we will look at a sample story dealing with each of them, but the principles involved apply to "growing-up" stories in general.

In order to write this sort of story, the precise nature of the problem must be considered. While parents may wish to help their child to change a troublesome pattern of behavior, in many cases some behavioral change is usually called for on the parents' side as well, and that should also be described in your story. This does not necessarily mean that the parents are wholly responsible for the behavior problem, although that can be the case. For example, some children who have difficulty separating are responding to an unconscious awareness of their parents' unresolved concerns about their independence and separateness.

When children have trouble with anger or stubbornness, their vulnerability (expressed simply by the fact that they have not "grown out of" this pattern as promptly as other children seem to) is often complicated by patterns of exchange between the parent and child. These patterns have become part of the problem, and a cycle of family behaviors may have arisen around them: Johnny can't control his temper; Mom has trouble managing his tantrums; Dad gets frustrated and spanks Johnny; Mom gets mad at Dad for failing to be patient; Mom gives Johnny a treat to help him to feel better. Now Johnny's problem has become a family problem, and everybody's behavior needs to be changed.

Parents should be reassured, however, that such changes are often easier to make than they might expect. Talking with other parents can help. Some parents experience a lot of guilt when they think about taking steps to modify their child's responses. They worry that the child "needs" to behave that way for some reason, or that their own motivations are selfish. But what sort of relationship is it, if your own feelings and needs are not taken into account, as well?

Children are usually very sensitive to the fact that certain behaviors drive their parents crazy. On the one hand, they are tempted to keep doing them, because they heighten their sense of their own power; but at the same time, they are left with a great deal of discomfort when they continue to do something that they know will make Mom and Dad mad.

"You need to boss your body" is a frequently heard phrase at the therapeutic preschool program where I am a consultant. Many of these children have problems with regulating their activity levels or their anger. We work with them by showing, in very specific ways, how to "boss" themselves and feel proud. It does not feel good to be out of control.

Children who have problems with self-control are often somewhat oppositional as well. They cannot trust themselves or their behavioral controls. It seems easier and safer for them to say NO! than to try and to fail. They need to understand that if they can learn to boss themselves (instead of other people), they will not be bossed as much by adults, and also that when they fail to do so, adults will have to step in and do it for them.

Another frequently heard expression is "Use your words." This requires patience, but the more children can rely on their language skills, the more they can use words instead of "acting out" in response to difficult situations. Children are usually aware of when they have difficulty "bossing themselves" or "using words," and it affects their sense of pride. In even very young children, self-judgment is possible. After all, the earliest acts of coordination (walking, crawling, grabbing a ball) require observation, self-evaluation, and then refinement of the particular behavior. By the age of four, this pattern can be observed when children try to draw. They exclaim, "That doesn't look right!" and clearly exhibit internal standards of how things should be. The same process goes on with behavioral patterns at an even earlier age. Children have an idea of how they should act, and some critical awareness of how they actually *do* act, even before they acquire the self-control to change their behavior.

For these reasons, defining and describing the problematic behavior in simple terms is the parents' first task. It also makes up the first part of the story. Clarifying what the new behavior should be is the second part. For the third, the parents should describe the new steps *they* need to take in order to reinforce and support the child's changes. The story should explain all of this clearly and consistently.

Our next story is for a child who is having tantrums. For some children, this is a natural developmental phase. But not all children have tantrums, and some of those who do have more intense tantrums than others. Tantrums most often occur during the terrible two's and tend to disappear by the third birthday. They are part of the process called "separation and individuation."

All children need to learn that they are separate, autonomous individuals, with a life and a will of their own. The ability to say "yes" or "no" is a major step in that learning. It is not simply a cognitive process; it is deeply emotional, and this is both normal and important. The "yes" and the "no" need to be integrated with the child's feelings. "Yes" comes to be associated with willed affirmation, while "no" is a rejection of whatever feels like "not me" to the child. "No" is also an affirmation of the child's ability to reject parental control and yet survive the parents' disappointment and anger.

At the same time, social and emotional standards of behavior are being learned. Just because a child can now say "no" does not mean that parents should always accept that answer. "No" can be tolerated as part of the learning process, but at the same time, the child should also learn that "no" is neither called for nor possible all the time. The child can learn that the parents will still love and protect, and will accept the child's different and separate self, but that they will not go along with the natural, but totally self-centered, concept of "I only want to do what I want, when I want to do it."

The process of normal social training involves children learning to take into account the needs and norms of their social context. Children can be autonomous, but they are also social creatures. The need for social training does not end when your child has passed through those terrible two's; adolescents have to struggle with learning it all over again at yet another level. The balance between freedom and responsibility is difficult to strike, and how to do that is best learned in the various developmental levels of childhood.

Parents begin to help their children with this emotional lesson when they teach them to say "yes" and "no" as preschoolers. If a child is still having difficulty with it at the age of three, a special story might do the trick:

No More Trantrums for Me!

page 1: I used to get so mad.
page 2: I would make a mad face and stamp my feet.
page 3: I hated that word, NO!
         When I asked for a cookie before supper, I heard No!

When I said I would put dirt in Suzie's hair, I heard No!

When I was pulling the dog by his tail, Mommy and Daddy said: NO!

page 4: I would get so mad. Sometimes I would lie down on the floor and kick and scream. Mommy would say I was having a tantrum. She would yell, and give me a spank.

This is the *beginning* of the book. It describes and defines the problem. The description is about mad feelings, not about being bad. The child needs to know that his parents understand this distinction. It is also worth emphasizing that the child has these feelings with both Mommy and Daddy. Mad feelings have to do with the No word, and that can come from anyone the child is close to. Perhaps examples with peers (when someone won't share a toy) or with a teacher or grandparent could be included. The child can recall some of these events, with a parent's help. This may also be a good place for the parents to review their own guidelines for the use of the word "no" with the child, and exactly what rules they are attempting to convey. Subtle (or not so subtle) differences between the parents may need to be explored and settled. The clearer the parents are about all of this, the clearer it will be for the child.

Finally, the child's behavior is described in a neutral way, not condemned. It is given a name: a *tantrum.* If the word can be conveyed simply as a description of the behavior, and not as an accusation, the child can use it to overcome that behavior. Eventually, in the course of the story, he will learn what the new routine will be when tantrums occur.

page 5: But I'm going to learn something new.

page 6: I can use my words.

page 7: I can tell Mommy and Daddy when I'm mad. I can say, "I don't like that" or "That's too hard" or "Not now." Then Mommy and Daddy can tell me about other choices. We can all use our words.

That is the middle of the story. It conveys two very simple messages. The first is that the child is going to learn how to use words when he feels mad. The second is that Mommy and Daddy are going to use their words, too, and help the child to make a different choice. For instance, when the child asks for cookies before supper, the choice can be: "You can have a carrot now while you are waiting, or we can put some cookies on a special plate for you to have after supper." When a friend doesn't want to play, he can be helped to say, "I don't like that," and other activities can be explored. When the dog's tail is being pulled, he can learn a new way to pat the dog, or play a pretend game of pulling a stuffed animal's tail.

If a pattern of escalating tantrums has evolved in the family, it should be interrupted. The story reminds the parent as well as the child that *everyone* is going to learn to use their words.

page 8:   Sometimes I still have trouble bossing my mad feelings.

page 9:   When my little sister took my ball, I pushed her down. When Mommy said no, I had a tantrum. I forgot to use my words.

page 10: Mommy sent me to my yellow chair to have a time-out. I didn't want to go to my yellow chair, I wanted to play with my ball. Mommy said she knew that. After I had my time out, I could play with my ball again.

page 11: Mommy told Suzie to use her words if she wanted my ball.

page 12: Then Mommy and I read my book about mad feelings together again. There are lots of times when I can use my words.

This is the *end* of the story. It reinforces the messages and reminds the child that this new lesson is not going to be learned immediately. It describes a new routine for tantrums: The mad feelings will be understood; the child will be told again about using words instead; there will be a brief (one-minute) time-out in a designated chair; the child will then be allowed to return to the activity of choice. The story also carries a reminder that other members of the family need to use their words, too. His little sister has to give up the ball because she did not use her words to get it. And the warmth and comfort of storytime acts as a reassurance as well as a chance to talk about learning a new behavior.

The next story addresses a situation in which parents may be more concerned about a child's sad or scared feelings.

I Go to Bed by Myself with My Teddy

page 1: I want a drink of water!

page 2: Daddy, come lie down with me!

page 3: Mommy, I'm scared! Can you change the light again?

page 4: These are the things I call out from my bed after Mommy and Daddy give me a kiss goodnight. They come and do them for me because I am crying.

The *beginning* of this story, as in the story about tantrums, describes the child's current feelings and what goes on at bedtime. It does not place blame or make accusations. Whatever the child's behavior, it should be described, as should the parents' responses. If the parents respond erratically—sometimes with sympathy, sometimes with silence, or even sometimes with angry shouts—this should be admitted.

page 5: Sometimes Daddy feels sad for me and comes in and lies down with me. Sometimes Daddy feels mad and yells, "Go to sleep!"

Parents can have difficulty with a settled bedtime routine because the child has a tendency to be anxious at times of separation, or because the parent feels a little guilty about not fully attending to the child's "needs" at the moment. Often, both are the case. The point here is to establish a new routine that can help the child to contain the anxious feelings, and also permit the parent to feel comfortable about what is being provided during the transition to sleep.

page 6: Mommy and Daddy say running around at my bedtime makes them mad and sad. They have other jobs to do. They need to have talks with each other, just like they have talks with me.

page 7: Mommy and Daddy say we're going to do something new. Each night we will have time to get a drink, have some company, and fix my light. After supper, I'll take my bath. Then we'll have storytime. I'll get my Teddy to keep me company in bed. I can tell him stories and share a toy with him until we fall asleep.

page 8: Mommy and Daddy will take turns helping me. We're going to make a calendar for when it's Mommy's turn and when it's Daddy's turns.

The middle of the book introduces the new messages, and the parents' feelings about the child's predicament are more fully described. The child needs to know that, besides empathic concern, some irritation was aroused. This section should show that they are all members of a family system, and that the behavior of one does, indeed, affect the others. It tells the child (and when children are three years old, it is time they begin to understand this) that his Mommy and Daddy are also each other's husband and wife. This means they have other jobs to do, such as caretaking that relationship.

Having other relationships *does* mean having more jobs; it does not mean that the child is being deserted. Everyone in a family has to struggle with the question of what is an equitable allotment of time and attention, and everyone has to try to make room in their hearts and minds and schedules for everyone else.

All too often, this task of "making room" has fallen solely on the woman in the family, producing a distortion in society that many men and women have been attempting to address in recent years. Men are beginning to learn that their lives are hollow when focused solely on achievement in the realm of work, without real emotional investment in meaningful relationships. While most women are well aware of that particular risk, they run others of their own, in the belief that they should be "superwomen" and try to have it all. Building stories for children that touch on such issues is a good way to begin to prepare them to cope eventually with life's larger dilemmas by providing some first words for the ideas and the feelings.

The second message in this bedtime story is that something new is going to be attempted. The schedule for the new bedtime routine is laid out, with a calendar promised to help structure the child's expectations. The child's stated needs (water, light, company) are provided for. If some further requests are made later on, the book can be modified accordingly with another page.

page 8: If I do a good job getting Teddy and me to sleep, then Mommy and Daddy can rest and feel good. I'll feel proud.

page 9: When I wake up, I can look at my door. If I have a star on my chart, I'll know that Mommy or Daddy will read me a book before breakfast.

The end of the story adds a behavioral reinforcer. Because this new change will result in some stress—as is always the case when any behavior in a family is changed—attention should be paid to making sure that everyone gets some reward. For this child, the time that used to be spent struggling over bedtime can become a special sharing time in the morning, instead. Obviously, this means a change in parental schedules, too, but the benefits of the new arrangement should be for everyone to share.

Children feel proud when they take a step forward in developing behavioral controls, and it is important for them to know that Mommy and Daddy will help them to conquer fears and insecurities as well as troublesome behaviors. But we all need to remember that children get ready for different developmental steps at different times. It used to be that most pediatricians and parents believed there was a certain proper age when all children should be required to give up such things as thumbsucking or a blankie. Fortunately, parents are now encouraged to accept their own child's internal pacing. There are still times, however, when developmental steps get imposed on a child by the demands of the environment, for instance, when they need to say goodbye to a blankie because it is time to start going to school.

Both parents and children feel pushed and pulled at once by such impositions. Children are sad about losing their old place within the family, while at the same time they can be glad about their new school. Parents can feel guilty about depriving their children of favored routines or habits, but they also want them to move on and "get bigger." Parents can be scared, too, for both themselves and for their children, of "what-next?" This is something that every family must struggle with during a child's development, from infancy through adolescence.

Some changes are demanded, not by your child's developmental requirements, but by events in the family or in a parent's work schedule. Children can be confused about what will happen next, and whether or not a parent will be available. Their memories are supported by familiar things in their environment, and when these change, they may suffer from both loss and disorientation. Whether the change is as minor as a new babysitting arrangement, or as major as beginning nursery school or daycare, parents need to spend time preparing their children. For even larger scale changes, affecting the entire family (a move across town, or across the continent), parents have to help children say goodbye to the old without disrupting their sense of security or overwhelming them with loss.

As adults, we often have to consciously put aside other mental agendas in order to be present in the here-and-now, but children's sense of time is very concentrated. They live naturally in the moment. When children walk down the street and find a leaf, a piece of discarded gum, or a strangely shaped stone, the rest of the world—as well as the mother who is trying to get them home from the daycare center—simply disappears. Just as such moments of scientific curiosity can absorb a child completely, so too can a moment of frustration. For these reasons, change is especially difficult for younger children. Their worries about a new event are not readily balanced by an ability to recall "the big picture."

Research has shown that children adjust to daycare more readily when younger than nine months than they do between nine and fifteen months. The reason seems to be that increased ability to discriminate changes in their surroundings leads to more stress. At an early age, babies are very accepting of any caretaker who meets their needs. Later they have a clearer picture in their memory of their usual cast of characters and of their routines. This should remind us how actively the child is involved with the world, even before the ability to communicate about it exists.

Playful rituals make a game of change and diminish anxiety. As soon as toddlers are able to use the helpful phrase "Be back!" homemade books can help remind them that Mommy and Daddy will indeed return. Words and pictures can come together to help give some structure to their experiences, so they will not be overwhelmed by change. Pictures can help with remembering new people or places and, once they can use them, words will help with their feelings.

For the first two years of life, pictures and objects are the most important helpers. Bringing along familiar blankets or toys helps to establish a sense of connection with a change in the environment. Similarly, bringing home something the child made or played with at daycare or the babysitters affirms the connection between the two settings, giving the child a sense of security.

By eighteen months (and even sooner for some children), simple storybooks can be of help. One of these might begin with a snapshot collage on the refrigerator door of "My Babysitters." As care increasingly moves outside the home, pages of babysitters, teachers, school activities, or where Mommy and Daddy work can grow into a picturebook about "My Days."

AN ALBUM TO EMPHASIZE PEOPLE

A simple photo album divided into sections can help children accept having someone new take care of them. It emphasizes the idea that other people besides their parents are already part of their lives:

SECTION 1: These are people in my family.
SECTION 2: These are people who help Mommy and Daddy.
SECTION 3: Here I am having fun with grown-ups.
SECTION 4: Grown-ups help me, too.
SECTION 5: Here I am playing with my friends.
SECTION 6: Here are my new friends and new helpers.

For that last section, an advance trip to the nursery school or daycare center will give you the pictures you need. The trip can also be used to give your child an opportunity to see the new setting for himself, and to return home with some concrete reminders of it, in the photographs.

A CALENDAR TO EXPLAIN THE NEW ROUTINE

A color-coded calendar on the wall can help kids to know what is going on: blue for school days, for instance, yellow for weekends, purple for special trips or visits. You can also help them to make scrapbook pages for each kind of day, with pictures of schools and parks and other children for blue days, family friends on yellow ones, and Grandma and Grandpa's impending visit highlighted in purple.

A MAP TO SHOW ALL THE PLACES

The best preparation for a new nursery school is a series of brief visits beforehand, on a variety of days and at different times, including lunch and nap time. These little trips can lead to making a map with your child. A big oak-tag sheet can be used to show where home is, where the child's new school is, where any brothers or sisters go to school, where Mommy and Daddy work. Landmarks can be drawn in, or snapshots of them pasted on.

Little children are not able to say, "I'm getting mixed up about what's going on here, and who's going to help me?" but parents can support their first steps toward independence and assuage their fears by clearly labeling and defining the comings and goings that are part of normal family life. Using simple language, you can tell a child that you know he is worried or angry when you leave him. It may indeed make him mad or sad when you say goodbye at the babysitter's or the daycare center, but he has to learn how to cope with the demands of family life at some point, and your sensitivity to his feelings should bolster his efforts to cope, not to retreat.

A NEW MOVE

The stabilizing influences of familiar territory, known friends, and nearby relatives are not easy to replace, and are often painful to lose. A move can disrupt the entire family, and a preschooler in particular. The network of relations that helps children feel secure can be threatened. What worries children most is the inevitable disruption within the family. Moves often require one or both parents going on preparatory trips. Sharing information with children is essential, and an "About My Move" book can provide an itemized list of what has happened and what will happen. Albums, maps, and calendars will also help children understand. A book called "The Many Places I've Been" can stress the positive features of the move: the opportunities to come to know different places and things.

But it is important to accept that children will still "act out" some of their discomfort (it should be noted that adults will sometimes do the same). They may tend to get angry over parts of their routines that had come to be accepted, like getting dressed in the morning, and they may cry louder and more often over little deprivations. There may be temper tantrums where there were none before. Because children often have difficulty knowing consciously that "it'll be sad to miss your friend Jimmy," they may need help to recognize their distress. The "About My Move" book can define these natural feelings, creating an opportunity for children to identify and vocalize their concerns.

The Many Places I Have Been Book

page 1: The Many (this is many; this is a few)
page 2: Places I Have Been Book
page 3: I'm Christopher
page 4: I'm four – 1, 2, 3, 4
page 5: I have a Mommy,
page 6: a Daddy, and a Dog

The first pages are used to establish the basics for the child. An introduction is made to the main idea (the places) and the child's security (the family). The child's adventures are introduced positively.

page 7:   Let me show you something – LOOK
page 8:   A car, a boat, a bus, a plane. These are different rides I have taken.
page 9:   The city, the suburbs, the country. These are different places I have been.
page 10: Do you want to know why?
page 11: When I was a little baby (waa, waa)
page 12: I lived in the city, with tall buildings,
page 13: and traffic, and lots of people.
page 14: Then my Daddy got a new job. (This is Daddy.)
page 15: We said goodbye to Grandpa and Grandma. (Everybody cried a little.) We waved goodbye and we went to live in the country. We rode on an airplane, like the one I showed you.

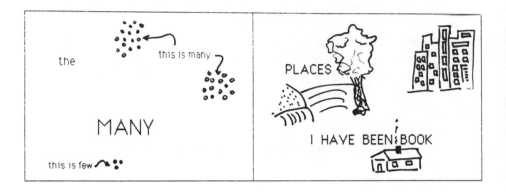

the

this is many

MANY

this is few

PLACES

I HAVE BEEN BOOK

I'M CHRISTOPHER

I'M FOUR

1 2 3 4

I have a Mommy

a Daddy

and a dog

Then my Daddy got a NEW JOB. (Daddys can do that a lot.) We had to move again.

We took a long ride in the car across the country.

We got a big house in the suburbs. There were shopping centers

There were houses and lawns and snow in the wintertime.

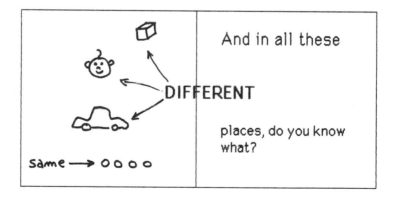

Same → O O O O

And in all these

DIFFERENT

places, do you know what?

SOMETHING

has always been the

SAME! oooo

Guess what?

Me

MOM DAD

and my family and my dog.

a smile

We are a happy family.

We can go lots of different places together.

page 16: Then I lived in the country. There were fields,
page 17: and farm animals, and lots of sunshine!

A simple explanation is given to the child. Information is presented in a simple way. It is designed to help the child organize life events he or she has experienced. The feelings associated with the move are acknowledged with sympathetic acceptance.

page 18: Then my Daddy got a New Job. (Daddys can do that a lot.) We had to move again.
page 19: We took a long ride in the car across the country.
page 20: We got a big house in the suburbs. There were houses and lawns.
page 21: There were shopping centers, and snow in the wintertime.

Places are treated positively, as if they all offered opportunities for the child and family. Then the child is led toward a conclusion. And the basic security of the child is reaffirmed.

page 22: And in all these DIFFERENT places,
page 23: do you know what?
page 24: SOMETHING has always been the SAME! Guess what?
page 25: Me and my family and my dog.
page 26: We are a happy family.
page 27: We can go lots of different places together.

For older children, particularly, a move means disruption of special peer relationships, but no child is too young to feel the pain of no longer being close to someone special. A book can address the way friends can stay friends, even when far apart. Telephone contact can be pictured, and practice calls made.

Young children's worries can be compounded by concerns for their own special things. You can help them to pack their things in their own boxes, and give them time to decide what will travel with them and what gets put into the boxes. Letting them mail something to themselves at your present address will reassure them that whatever gets "shipped away" can, indeed, come back. Space should also be set aside in memory for the "old place," even while children are preparing for the new. A book can describe what was special in the first residence, as well as what is intriguing about the new one. It can emphasize that the whole family is embarking together on a new and exciting adventure!

< 7 >

Stories About
Illness and Death

It should be clear by now that this book advocates a straightforward, but gentle, sharing of reality. Children may experience some stress as a result of facing a potentially unpleasant event, but their stress can be much greater when they are not informed, and a lack of sharing can create barriers between parents and children. When poorly prepared for events in the life of the family, a child's apprehension about everything else can increase alarmingly. It is like "waiting for the other shoe to drop."

By the time a child is two, she may be able to remember many events, and she is also beginning to classify whether these experiences were "good" or "bad." Children need help with tolerating "bad" things until their perspectives broaden. One of the earliest exchanges of this sort involves visits to the doctor. The parent can admit that sometimes seeing the doctor is "no fun" and discuss, in a simple way, the degree to which the child has felt some apprehension in the past. Additional education can include providing play-doctor kits or hospital figures to facilitate the child's communication about her feelings. How the next visit may be different from earlier ones should be explained beforehand. Parents can also point out which parts of this new visit to the doctor might be fun.

Children are naturally curious, and this can be used to prepare them for learning more about themselves and their bodies. They can begin to see going to the doctor's office as a way to keep healthy as they get bigger. Much of what happens in a doctor's office does have to do with the child's growth, after all. Children love having a marker on the wall at home that shows their height at each birthday; they can also feel excited about another opportunity to show their doctor how much bigger they have become. But what can happen at the doctor's is not limited to being weighed and measured, so you should think about what else needs to be explained beforehand. The following list suggests explanations that can help develop a positive attitude:

Measuring blood pressure. A child can learn that this is how the doctor makes sure that the heart is doing a good job of pushing the blood and all the body's helpers (food and oxygen) around to all the different parts of the body.

Doctors' lights. These are for looking at all the tiny places, in their eyes, ears and mouth. Practicing at home with a flashlight can prepare children to sit still for this. The child may want a turn to do it to you.

Stethoscopes. These allow doctors to hear all the sounds the heart makes, and how the air goes in and out of your lungs. Your child can listen to your heart and lungs without a stethoscope, just by pressing her ear against your chest.

Hands. Doctors use their hands to feel children's arms, legs, and tummies. Sometimes they poke with their fingers here and there; sometimes it tickles.

Needles. Doctors use needles to help them to look at your blood, to make sure it is healthy. Sometimes doctors use needles to give you injections to help your body fight off germs that can make you sick. Needles don't feel good. They can make you say ouch! Can you practice saying *ouch?*

A book about visiting the doctor should begin with a simple introduction to how the child's body works. It can then explain what the doctor will do to make sure that everything is okay. Finally, the child's mad or sad feelings about getting a shot can be mentioned, and the reward the child will get for sitting still can be made into a mystery ending.

A Visit to the Doctor

page 1: This is my body. I have hands and feet. I have eyes and ears.

page 2: I'm getting big. I'm going to show the doctor how big my body is.

page 3: The doctor will want to see all the different parts of me. She'll even want to check things that I can't see.

page 4: She has special lights, and special tools to help check my body. She even has a special camera (called an X-ray machine) that can take pictures of my bones. She has a stethoscope (Can you say that?) and a little hammer to knock on my knees and elbows.

page 5: My body has parts to help me grow. My stomach holds the food I eat. Do you think the doctor can feel what I ate for breakfast? Let's see if she can.

page 6: My heart goes thump-thump. It's strong. My lungs go whoosh-whoosh. Can you hear them?

page 7: My brain helps me learn words and do lots of jobs. The doctor may ask me to do different jobs for her. I might have to stand on my tippy toes, or guess what color she holds up.

page 8: Sometimes my doctor tells me she needs to take a little blood or has to give me a shot. I might feel a little scared, but Mom (or Dad) will hold my hand. I have to sit very still. I might cry a little. It's really a big job to sit so still.

page 9: Can you guess what I did after I went to the doctor's office? I felt proud. Mom wanted me to feel happy for trying to sit still. Even though I cried, she said I did a good job.

If there are other examinations that your child may have to undergo, do not hesitate to ask the doctor's office about them before the appointment. Knowing what to expect will allay a great deal of your own anxiety, as well as your child's. Everyone will be more comfortable if you know what to expect. For children younger than three years old, though, extended preparation for medical visits can make them worry more, rather than less. They will do best if given the information only a day or two in advance.

Any medical visit is also a good time to introduce children to general information about and pictures of their bodies. They can begin to learn names for different body parts, both inside and out. By the age of three, most children are able to grasp the concept of the brain, the heart, the lungs, and the gastrointestinal tract.

Books aren't the only useful approach to preparing a child for seeing the doctor. Play-doctor kits are a great help. They allow children to get used to the different instruments that may be used. They can try them out on Mommy or Daddy, on friends or toys. They can practice giving shots as well as getting them. You may notice that some of your child's anger about being subjected to the doctor's visit will be shown in the vigor with which she gives *you* a shot. She may also be quite intrusive with the stethoscope or flashlight. Some limits may need to be set. Your child may need to be reminded that the doctor does not like to hurt kids, but shots are one of the ways that medicine has to be given sometimes to make them well. Let your child know that you understand that going to the doctor's office can make her a little scared or mad. You can also help her to realize that sitting still is a "big job," but it allows the doctor to be done quicker.

Similar preparation should be done for a visit to the dentist. Help your child know what to expect. Tell her what the different tools are that the dentist will use. Watching someone else be examined can help, too. Let her accompany you whenever you go to the doctor or dentist for a routine examination. The fact that everyone has to do it should make it a little easier when her turn comes. Children can learn a great deal from watching how those around them handle situations.

HOSPITAL CARE

A visit to the doctor or the dentist is, of course, less traumatic than a stay at a hospital. Especially for children younger than four, stress and anxiety are a normal part of a hospital stay, and the sort of preparations we have been discussing are only a small part of what they need to get through it. Fortunately, more and more hospitals have accommodations for parents to "live in." A caring adult's presence, voice, and touch are what is most helpful. (This holds true through adolescence, and adulthood, too, for that matter; some basic needs are not ever "grown out of.")

Some hospitals allow children and parents to visit beforehand, while others have special programs on videotape showing admission procedures. Some offer personnel trained to help the child to understand what is going on. Most children's floors also have special toys and places to play. You can point out to your child that staying at the hospital does not mean she can't have *any* fun.

Involving your child in small choices will allow her to feel some sense of control. You can, for example, ask which pajamas she would like to take along, and which special toys. This can even be done with some medical procedures. You or the nurse can ask which arm a shot should go into, or whether the child wants to have her temperature taken standing up or sitting down.

It helps your child to know some of the whys and wherefores. The medical problem should be explained in simple terms, and the child should be told how the doctors and nurses will be working together to help her. This means that you will have to know all these things yourself. It is difficult to comfort a child when you are confused and anxious. Parents should always respect their own need to have good medical information.

You will help your child get used to being in the hospital most by spending time with her when she is there. After the initial adjustment to the hospital routine, the days and hours when Mom, Dad, relatives, and friends will visit should be marked on a calendar. Much of the anxiety that children can experience in a hospital stay has to do with their need to be reassured of a continued caring presence.

THE BOOK-AND-BUNNY APPROACH

One technique to help a child manage an illness is a combined book-and-stuffed-animal approach. The toy I selected for one child was a bunny. The book I wrote was called "The Sick Bunny Book." The child was told that the animal had the same illness as she did, and needed to go along in order to get the same treatment. All the tests and needles were tried out on the bunny first. The child read the book I wrote for her with the bunny. She explained to the bunny what was wrong and what was going to happen to both of them. Listening in on some of these conversations she had with her toy gave her parents a chance to note, and to correct, many of her misperceptions.

In a child's play with the "sick" stuffed animal, there should be room for fantasy as well as information. Often children don't like to play out situations in one-to-one correspondence. They may invent their own hospital and their own rules. All the nurses may be dragons that bite little children, and all the doctors may be monsters. Some of this play can be accepted, and does not call for correction. It is simply a way of saying that things are tough in the hospital. After all, the sick bunny cannot feel good all the time. In fact, that bunny may be sad and mad during much of the child's stay. When the stay lengthens to a week or more, the discomfort level rises.

"The Sick Bunny Book" is a way to give the child a chance to be in charge. The stuffed toy will have to do as the child says. Even if the bunny fusses, too bad! The child will do whatever needs to be done. Depending upon the child's interest, new pages can be made daily at the hospital, to keep the story up-to-date.

The Sick Bunny Book

page 1: Once upon a time, a little bunny got sick.
page 2: He didn't feel very well. The little bunny got sad.

The beginning of the book stresses that when illness strikes, it is natural to feel sad and bad.

page 3: Mommy and Daddy Bunny stayed with him.
page 4: They decided to call Doctor Rabbit.
page 5: Doctor Rabbit said the little bunny had to have tests and get needles.
page 6: Sometimes the little bunny was sad.
page 7: Sometimes the little bunny was mad.
page 8: Sometimes the little bunny was scared.

The little bunny has a lot of different feelings about being sick. There is room to attach specific events to each feeling to help the child understand.

page 9: Doctor Rabbit says: Little Bunny has to have shots. Can you give him his shots?
page 10: The little bunny says: That makes me mad, but I have to hold still.
page 11: Doctor Rabbit says: Little Bunny has to take medicine. Can you give him his medicine?
page 12: The little bunny says: That makes me sad. The medicine is yucky, but I have to take it.
page 13: Doctor Rabbit says: Little Bunny needs to have more tests. Can you tell him about his tests?
page 14: The little bunny says: That makes me scared, but Mommy and Daddy give me hugs.

What the little bunny has to put up with in order to get better is emphasized, not just his feelings.

The

SICK BUNNY

BOOK

Once upon a time, a little
bunny got sick.

He didn't feel very well
and the little bunny got sad.

Mommy and Daddy Bunny stayed with him.

They decided to call Doctor Rabbit.

Doctor Rabbit said little bunny had to have tests and get needles.

Sometimes little bunny was sad.

Sometimes little bunny was mad.

Sometimes little bunny was scared.

Doctor Rabbit says little bunny has to have shots. Can you give him his shots?

Little bunny says that makes me mad But I have to hold still.

Doctor Rabbit says little bunny has to take medicine. Can you give him his medicine?

Little bunny says that makes me sad. The medicine is ycchy but I have to take it.

Doctor Rabbit says little bunny needs to have more tests. Can you tell him about his tests?

Little bunny says that makes me scared. But Mommy and Daddy can give me hugs.

CAN YOU HELP LITTTLE BUNNY FEEL BETTER?

BLANKIE

BANDAIDS

TOYS

ICE CREAM

page 15: Can you help Little Bunny feel better? (pictures of
blankie, bandaids, toys, ice cream)

The last page is set up to encourage the child to think about
the things that may, at times, make Little Bunny feel better.
It is an open invitation to talk during a period of stress.

SERIOUS ILLNESSES

"A Little Boy's Battle with Bad Cells" was originally written
to help a preschooler deal with leukemia. It can also be used
for children with cystic fibrosis, diabetes, or any severe disease.
It was meant to be a rallying cry for the child, to foster optimism and a "fighting attitude" in order to keep him involved
in the struggle against the exhaustion, apathy, and despair
that can come with chronic illness.

Children can accept that their bodies may have made a
"mistake." They know how easy it is to "mess up" in a variety
of ways, so it is not a great leap of the imagination to the
notion that some part of their body has gotten into "a mess."
Children do not usually experience such ideas as either a
value judgment or a direct blow to their self-esteem. They
seem quite able to think of parts of themselves separately.
Just as they can get mad at their hands for going the wrong
way when they are trying to make a painting, they can
understand that their lungs (as in asthma) or the part of their
body that makes insulin (as in diabetes) or some enzymes (as
in cystic fibrosis) are not doing the right thing. They can
accept that doctors can help their bodies do a better job, even
though this means they will have to put up with all the
aggravating things that doctors may ask of them.

It is both acceptable and understandable when anger
sometimes gets focused on procedures, medicines, or even
certain hospital personnel, but limits need to be set on such
anger if it begins to interfere with cooperation in medical
procedures. It is fine for the child to say "I hate my yucky
medicine" or "That stupid nurse makes me mad," but it is

another matter to refuse to take the medicine, or to prevent that nurse from doing what needs to be done. When parents understand that the free expression of anger is compatible with compliance in the "hard jobs," it is easier for the child all around.

We all use a little bit of denial (It's not *so* bad) when troublesome things occur, but complete denial (This isn't happening) can block acceptance of both the illness and the adjustments that may be needed for successful treatment. Children are often able to muster exactly the right amount of optimism and denial by themselves. Since childhood is the introduction to life experience, children do not have many preconceived notions of what has to be. They can feel that being stuck with an illness "isn't fair," but they can usually also find a good blend of acceptance. Children can manage whatever it may be that they are "stuck with" as long as they can stretch themselves. They want to do everything a "normal child" can, to go as far as they would like, and not to be overprotected. This natural accommodation is facilitated by appropriately measured doses of information, so that children do not get too confused by what is going on around them.

But children are often confused and distressed by the family's fears, lack of acceptance, or anger at the doctors for not being able to make everything better. For this reason, parents need to examine their own feelings and reactions when their child is ill. Parental attitudes can determine more of a child's adjustment than any other aspect of the illness. This does not mean, however, that parents should deny that the child's illness makes them sad, or even a little frightened.

Sickness does not make anybody happy, and kids know this, so it is alright if Mommy and Daddy cry sometimes. Children will even try to comfort their parents. They have a natural sympathy for those they love, and they also need to protect their source of security (their parents) for their own reasons. They still need reassurance that the family team can keep working together with the doctors to do the best that can be done, and that their parents' full support will be available in those moments when their own coping skills are overwhelmed.

"A Little Boy's Battle with Bad Cells" was designed to remind the child that, even though there are times that can be overwhelming (such as when the little boy is too tired to play or winds up crying), the objective is recovery. The hope is that recovery or remission will permit the child to play and have fun again. Realistic optimism helps all of us do the best we possibly can in painful situations. Helping the child to appreciate The Story That Is Life usually allows the natural coping mechanisms that children have to deal productively with feelings. It does not demand that we do more than we are able to do. Realistic optimism simply encourages us to do as much as we possibly can with the resources we have at the moment, "to be in the world while we are here."

A Little Boy's Battle with Bad Cells

page 1: This is a book about a little boy who lives with his Mommy and Daddy.
page 2: He liked to play, and suck his thumb, and drink apple juice.
page 3: One day, he did not feel good. His Daddy took him to the doctor's office. The little boy had a blood test. He said, "Ouch."
page 4: The doctor looked and looked at the blood test. "Oh, no," he said, "there are *bad* cells here. We have to chase them away."

The child is introduced to what it was like before there was a sickness. The circumstances of how the illness was discovered are explained. The child is prepared for the idea that there is a job to do. Bad cells have to be chased away. (Or the child's body needs extra helpers, like insulin).

page 5: "Go away, bad cells," said the doctor.
page 6: "Go away, bad cells," said the little boy.
page 7: "Go away bad cells," said the mommy and daddy.
page 8: But the doctor, and the little boy, and the mommy

and daddy needed helpers to chase the bad cells
away. They needed: more X- rays, more needles,
more nurse helpers.

The theme of everyone wanting the bad cells to go away and
for the little boy to be better is established. The new "jobs" that
will need to be done are introduced.

page 9:   "Ugh! Ugh! Ouch! Ouch!" said the little boy, and he
            cried.
page 10:   Sometimes the bad cells made the little boy feel so
            bad that he couldn't play.
page 11:   But then the doctor and nurse could help. Here is the
            medicine to make those bad cells go away.
page 12:   Mommy and Daddy and the little boy
page 13:   and Grandma and Grandpa and the doctor and the
            nurse all yelled together:
page 14:   "MAKE THOSE BAD CELLS GO AWAY!"

The pain and discomfort of treatment are acknowledged. The
bad feeling from the sickness are accepted, too. Hope and
family togetherness are emphasized. A positive outcome is
predicted.

page 15:   Little by little, the medicine chased the bad cells away.
page 16:   Everybody helped so that the little boy could begin
            to play again.

PAINFUL SITUATIONS

Any loss in the family brings parents, as well as children,
closer to the basic feelings that all of us must experience,
sooner or later. It reminds us that parents can only help their
children deal with those issues that they have settled, to some
degree, in their own lives. Those five basic feelings (glad, sad,
mad, scared, and "bad") that children experience are the same
ones that we all have to deal with, all our lives.

Parents cannot help their children manage angry feelings, if they cannot manage their own anger. If sadness leads you, as an adult, into denial or avoidance, how can you teach your child to accept sadness as an inescapable part of life? If feeling bad drags you into a depression, what tools can you offer for coping with the bad feelings that sometimes occur during school or play? When you have not been able to master your own fears and anxieties, how can you teach children to deal with being scared?

Parents may sometimes have the right words to explain things, but children always learn more quickly from observation—from the lesson of your deeds—than from words. Even before children have any words to describe events, they notice what happens. The logical explanations adults offer need a living reality to convince. Also, when parents have trouble having fun, it may be difficult for them to allow their children to be glad—then the natural exuberance of childhood may be constricted.

If violence, angry outbursts, or spankings are part of a child's everyday experience, telling her to "use your words" will have little impact. But if you can help your children with their words even when you are angry with them, your children will see that it *is* possible to talk about those mad feelings, after all, instead of hitting someone. Explanations will be an affirmation, not a cover-up.

This is not to say that managing emotions in life is easy. No one's family, no matter how well-adjusted, can avoid painful emotional experiences. Each individual must find a source of strength within herself. But the help that a family can provide in giving children words for their feelings and showing them how to cope with those feelings is invaluable.

Each book that parents make for their children, and the discussions each leads to, contributes to building that necessary strength of character. How children learn to cope with their basic feelings during their early years will stay with them for the rest of their lives. After all, the ability to manage anger and frustration is a requirement in the world of work. Taking on scary new assignments characterizes all stages of development. There will always be moments of self-doubt, confusion, or bad feeling that must be endured. Sadness or joy touch on many of life's events. Children can be prepared to accept these emotional experiences with calm understanding when they are offered the preparation early in life.

The closer these feelings come to "home"—to our most intimate relationships—the more this learning will be tested. Feelings are often most intense in the relationships that mean the most to us. These closest bonds directly affect our self-esteem as well as our self-confidence. Even when we have learned how to cope with our feelings in other life situations, it is still very difficult to apply what we have learned within the emotional cauldron of family life. However, acquiring the ability to manage major loss and disappointment during childhood can help to lay a foundation for such an achievement.

The ability to endure painful knowledge is solidified for children when, even in the midst of a parent's loss and suffering, that parent can make room to understand and to accept what the child is feeling. Then the child knows that, no matter what, her parents will attend to her needs. The family can care and comfort, even in times of stress. It may only require that (even though the child will have other caretakers for most of the day) you make certain that there is half an hour to talk and play together. Your child will learn that the pain can be endured.

A DEATH IN THE FAMILY

When the story parents have to write is about the loss of a significant person in their own life, as well as in their child's, all of their feelings, understanding, and values are brought to the forefront. Death makes children and adults think about a lot of things.

In the storybook, "Grandpa Died and I Feel Sad," a variety of tactics are used. The child's sadness is openly acknowledged. No attempt is made to cover it up. In fact, the pain is seen as part of the process with which an individual consolidates the good memories of the person who died. In this fashion, the relationship can continue, even though the person is gone. The parents' sadness is openly admitted, too. Crying is okay; it doesn't mean you're a baby. Some information is provided to help the child to understand that death is part of the scheme of things. The fact that death is also scary is mentioned, since children are inevitably reminded (as adults are) of their own mortality. Anger is accepted as a part of the experience of loss, as well. Losing someone is something nobody likes, and these feelings can be shared within the family.

This comforting, as the story explains, is not changed by special treats. Whether those are food, new toys, or a special diversion, they are less important than the act of sharing. The real comfort that parents offer their children is in their acceptance and love, and in their ability to listen to the child's bad feelings and to talk about them. This means offering the child genuine time in which the parent can be attentive to the things the child has to say.

Not every child is comforted by the same things. Some children like to be held and snuggled during talks about hard feelings. Others want to try to sit up by themselves before they allow physical contact. Parents should to be alert to the body language that children use as part of their message about what they are feeling. For younger or less verbal children, parents may need to provide the words, by careful questioning based on what they can sense of their child's reactions. Some children need time and prompting to be able to warm up to a topic. They seem to need the parents' words and permission to explore their own feelings. Others make an abrupt statement and then run away. Parents may need to find another time to show that they remember, and have been thinking about, the child's words, and to invite further discussion.

At the same time, parents need to be aware that they may be conveying, unintentionally, the message that it is *not* okay to talk about some things. Parents use body language, too, and it can tell a child that certain topics should be avoided. This may be because the topic is too painful (as it was for the Mommy in the Grandpa story), or it may derive from an assumption that children *shouldn't have to* deal with certain facts or feelings. But, unfortunately, children *do* have to deal, in some fashion, with what they are thinking and feeling.

Part of the current revolution in child psychology has been to demonstrate just how far-ranging children's ideas and feelings really are. Childhood is no longer seen as a golden age of happy thoughts. Children have to deal with stress, depression, and the unhappy facts of life whenever and wherever they encounter them. Most often, these encounters occur in the home. The fact that most child abuse (sexual or otherwise) is perpetrated by those closest to the victims is a stark reminder. And the same is true of most of the less blatant painful encounters. Their parents' behavior and attitudes, toward life and toward children, are closely observed and pondered by children, though not readily commented upon.

Children are very protective of their parents. Unless a great deal of support is offered, they will not tell their parent (let alone anyone else) when they feel that parent has made a mistake. The hurt is carried inside. Homemade books can be part of an effort to indicate that such painful topics can and should be openly discussed. Talking about traumatic events (even those caused by a parent's loss of patience or failure to understand) minimizes the trauma. It even contributes to the strength of child, and of the relationship with the parent, creating a space where communication and respect for each other's feelings are paramount.

Children have a real capacity for forgiveness, especially when they have seen that quality in action at home. It is possible for a parent to be angry, even when it is not justified, and to talk it over afterward, and for both parent and child to feel better. It is possible for a parent to be depressed and unavailable for a while, and for the child to accept this difficult fact. But this doesn't mean the child won't be angry! In fact, truly talking about the situation with the child means being able to be receptive to the child's "mad and sad and scared and bad" feelings about what happened. Just because the anger seems to be all over does not mean it has gone away. Everyone has some capacity to be able to forgive and forget. How much easier it is, though, when the situation has been acknowledged and an apology tendered. It is no different for children.

The processes with which they deal with loss are no different for children, either. Talking helps. In order for children to talk with parents, parents must be prepared to listen and to manage their own feelings. Death and loss underline how important it is to be receptive to your own feelings and to the messages you may be conveying, as well as to the various aspects of the child's feelings.

Grandpa Died and I Feel Sad

page 1: Grandpa died and I feel sad today.

page 2: I felt sad yesterday, too, and maybe I will tomorrow.

page 3: Mommy and Daddy say sad feelings are like when you say goodbye to someone.

page 4: Yesterday, I remembered when Grandpa used to play catch with me, and I felt sad.

page 5: (Grandpa's picture)

page 6: Today, I thought, when Grandma comes to visit, Grandpa won't be with her, and I felt sad.

page 7: Tomorrow, there is going to be a special party to say goodbye to Grandpa. I might feel sad then, too.

The topic of feelings is handled in a straightforward fashion, with no attempt to "cover-up" the pain. Sadness is the focus of these pages. It is important for the child to understand and accept that this sadness is natural. It will come and go at different times. A place is made for the positive memories that will trigger the sadness.

page 8:   Mommy helped me remember when Grandpa first got sick.

page 9:   He had to go to the hospital. Mommy cried a lot. She says it's OK when people cry when someone special is sick.

page 10: After Grandpa came out of the hospital, he couldn't play catch as much.

page 11: But Grandpa and I still had fun.
page 12: Then Grandpa got sick again. He had to stay in the
hospital a long time before he came home.
page 13: Then he died. Mommy cried when she told me.

These pages are used to help describe the situation of a lengthy illness. The Grandpa depicted is the mother's father. Simple details are shared. In the alternative pages below, the story describes the situation of a sudden death. Religious information may be included, too, as part of how the family understands nature's pain.

Alternative Pages

page 8: Daddy told me about dying when my goldfish died.
page 9: He said it was part of nature's plan to keep things
new, as the old leaves in the fall make way for
the new leaves in the spring.
page 10: I cried about my goldfish. I told Daddy I didn't like
nature's plan. It made me mad.
page 11: Daddy cried, too. He said some of nature's plan was
sad. He told me that when Grandpa died, he felt
sad and mad about nature's plan, too.
page 12: Sometimes nature's plan is a surprise. It happens all
of a sudden, like a thunderstorm.
page 13: We had just visited Grandpa last month, and then
we heard he died.

These alternative pages suggest that the subject of death, like other serious subjects, should be undertaken bit by bit with children. The fact that the child's goldfish was dead was discussed. It didn't just "go back to the sea through the toilet." And time was spent in helping the child to accept her feelings, and to learn a little more about life and life's experiences, including death.

page 14: When something dies, people feel sad.
page 15: Plants and fish and animals and people get old.
Then they die and we feel sad.

page 16: Sometimes things don't wait until they get old to die. That's scary.

page 17: Mommy and Daddy say that's an accident, and it doesn't happen much.

page 18: It mad me mad that Grandpa isn't going to visit anymore.

page 19: I asked for a special treat, but Mommy said it was too busy.

page 20: Daddy said sometimes special treats make sad feelings go away, but talking helps sad feelings go away better. Daddy said we'd have a special time together to talk about our feelings, like we always have. He cried a little.

page 21: Mommy cried, too. She said it was OK for me to tell her about my sad feelings even though she cried when we talked.

page 22: When we talk about Grandpa, we have special feelings and sad feelings, too.

page 23: Grandpa died and I feel sad. Mommy and Daddy say the sad feeling will go away little by little. The sad feeling helps us to remember all the special times with Grandpa better and better.

The end of the story emphasizes the healing power of sharing and the process of being able to recognize and accept feelings. Talking is seen as a way to better remember what someone has meant to a family.

It is always difficult to help a child deal with situations that arouse complex feelings in the adults concerned. Homemade books can help clarify guidelines of the important messages that a child may need to hear, but the effectiveness with which these messages are conveyed depends on parents' own emotional integrity, and on how well they have worked through their own feelings about the situation. The next two chapters confront parents again with the need to understand their own feelings, in dealing with divorce, adoption, and parental injury.

< **8** >

Stories About Divorce

The last chapter explored how parents need to maintain perspective while dealing with a child's pain, and how important it is for them to be able to identify their own feelings and to realize that their child's feelings may be quite different. In the issues we will focus on here and in the next chapter—divorce, adoption, and parental injury—those differences will be even greater. Books made for your children about them will require even more thought and self-awareness on your part than others we have discussed.

The conflict or estrangement in a marriage that can lead to separation often is not noticed by younger children. They focus primarily on what their parents mean to *them*. Adults should try to see their child's feelings through the lens he uses to view his world, not their own. And the earlier those feelings can be understood and discussed, the better.

Parents are usually able to sort out what it feels like for them to separate from their child at the daycare center or when he starts going to school, but in times of severe stress, they may have more trouble in differentiating their own feelings from those of the child. For this reason, the texts for these books will be examined more closely, to make it easier to understand how to help children deal with the issues involved.

The use of a sense of optimism as a part of that process will be described. A child can be encouraged to understand and accept a difficult situation while still looking on the bright side of things. In order to gain that perspective, however, children must first experience an acceptance of whatever feelings they have. In order to accept their children's feelings, parents need some distance from their own; otherwise, the parents' agenda can interfere with the child's mastery of these troublesome topics.

Parents should always remember that it is only husbands and wives who get divorced. Mommies and Daddies cannot divorce their children. Obviously, divorce represents a failure of communication between husband and wife. More and more, however, divorcing parents are willing to continue to work together for the best interests of their children.

The first version of our story about divorce is designed for parents who still have some ability to communicate with each other. First they need to decide together how best to share information with their children. The children will need reassurance from each parent to help them maintain their relationships with both. Supporting their children's ability to remain in touch not only with their positive but also with their negative feelings toward each parent will facilitate the best adjustment over time. (Sadly, since some parents still do desert their children or remain bitterly estranged, those possibilities will be considered in our second version of the story.)

When Mommy and Daddy Got Divorced

page 1: Mommy and Daddy told me that they aren't going to live together anymore. We had to have a family talk.

The bad news is announced immediately, on the assumption that the child has already heard some discussion of what has or is going to happen. Whenever possible, the mother and father should tell children this news together, and without blaming each other. This will help reassure a child that continuing to have a relationship with one of them will not be a betrayal of the other. Kids are often afraid that if Mommy and Daddy can get divorced from each other, they could get "vorced" from kids, too. Their uneasiness will be increased if they feel they have to choose who is the "good parent." Younger children, especially, are very sensitive to who is "good" and who is "bad," and it is hard for them to see both qualities in people at the same time. They need to believe that both Mommy and Daddy will still be there for them, even if there is a separation. A family talk about the coming changes will make such promises much more real.

Children also cannot help being worried about the anger and sadness each parent is feeling, and how it might affect their lives. They have probably already witnessed some unpredictability during the period of conflict preceding the announcement of a divorce. They should learn about what is going to take place *before* one or the other parent relocates, if possible. Page two lays the groundwork for sharing this information. There should be some time (at least a week) available for reviewing this news while that parent is still present. But the announcement should not be made too early. Younger children are very attentive to immediate realities. If told too far in advance that one parent is leaving, their wishes and fantasies for the family to stay together will take over again before the separation actually happens, and they will only be further confused.

page 2: Daddy will have a new place to live. I'm staying with Mommy, but Daddy's going to take one of my favorite teddy bears along to keep him company. I can sleep with Teddy when I go to visit him.
I'm going to visit his new house, and bring back a picture of Daddy and me there to put in this book.

This page assumes (as is still true in most cases) that it will be the father who establishes a new residence. Since mothers usually continue to function as the primary custodial parent, they most often remain in the original household with the children. Fathers have begun, in some instances, to assume this role, and sometimes two new residences are created. If this is the case, you can follow the suggestions given in the section on moves in Chapter 6. If at all possible, the separation and the move should be spaced at least a month apart, to minimize the amount of upheaval the child will need to deal with all at once. In any case, it is important to begin to share such information early in the story.

Page 2 has another function beyond establishing the reality of a new home for one parent. It underscores the fact that the departing parent is not leaving the child's life. The reality of their continuing relationship is symbolized by the child giving the parent some important object, a stuffed toy or a favorite blankie, to keep for him. The departing parent should also know what the child's favorite foods are, and should remind the child that these foods will be available at the new house, too. Some of the child's favorite clothing can also be kept there.

Visiting the new home will give the child a concrete sense of place and confirm that the parent is not going somewhere beyond the child's imagination. A photograph or something that caught the child's fancy at the new residence can be brought back to forge a further connection between the two places.

page 3: Mommy and Daddy are making a calendar for me of
          my different visits.

Page 3 emphasizes the importance of routine in helping the child to feel secure with the visitation arrangements. The sooner separating parents can create a reliable schedule, the better for all concerned. This will allay any fears the child may have of being caught in a game of divided loyalties. But it may take a little while for the child to believe in the new routine. He will probably want to know how his parents make these schedules, and he will be very concerned that they be kept. The child may become quite anxious at the slightest deviation, as well as before each visit.

Most young children, however, even in the face of such real disappointments as a visit canceled at the last minute, will keep up a positive front. They will share their tears and anger with the parent they live with if they are secure enough. But they may deny those same feelings when they speak to the visiting parent. They are likely to believe that their own thoughts or behavior caused the separation, and they will not want to risk further loss by revealing potentially hurtful sentiments.

When children behave like this, it is often very frustrating for the custodial parent, who may want to encourage the child to tell the other parent about the disappointing behavior, either to help the child to stand up for himself, or with a wish that the other parent will change. But neither of these motives is appropriate, in most cases, because it is usually too early for a child to "stand up to" either parent.

Unfortunately, it is also true that when parents behave in disappointing ways, they are often not particularly concerned about either the child's feelings or the repercussions of their behavior. A further complication would be for the custodial parent to urge the child to convey *her* hurt and anger, as well as the child's own. When missed visits occur often, it is usually a manifestation of the bitterness and embattled atmosphere that led to the divorce in the first place. Children, unfortunately, can still be pawns in this game, even after the final decree.

page 4: Mommy said I might go to a new school, because she's going to have to go to work.
If it happens, I'll have a chance to visit my new school first with both Mommy and Daddy.

If this sort of change is going to occur, it is important to share it as promptly as possible. The child's adjustment is made more difficult if each week brings more bad news. Children can tolerate a lot of change, as long as consideration continues to be given to letting them in on the story. If the child is going start daycare or a new school, both parents should visit with him beforehand. This further confirms his sense that both parents will continue to be concerned for his welfare. A visit to Mommy's new workplace, if possible, will help, too. Knowing where both parents are and what they are doing while the child is away at school is always reassuring.

page 5: I feel mad and sad. I wish Mommy and Daddy could change their minds.
I feel mad because I like my family the way it is.
I feel sad because things will be different.
Sometimes I just feel bad.

It is perfectly normal for a child to feel both mad and sad about the divorce. In fact, it is unavoidable. And these feelings need to be acknowledged and accepted. What makes the child sad can be explored in a nondefensive way. Being able to say to a child, "Yes, I know that Daddy not being at home makes you feel sad" is certainly better than "Big boys don't cry" (fostering denial) or "Daddy still visits—you shouldn't be sad" (which minimizes the child's feelings) or "Daddy was such a bum, I don't know how you could miss him" (a blaming reaction that complicates the child's ability to come to terms with what he may be feeling).

Once you are able to accept your child's sad feelings, you can ask for more detail in ways that can build a base for further communication: "What makes you so sad? I like to know about your feelings." True sharing helps children survive the stresses of growing up.

The angry feelings should be asked about, too, but will probably be harder for the child to describe. They may be acted out in misbehavior or refusal to comply with rules. In a healthy situation, these feelings will be directed at both parents, and both parents should be able to accept and understand that this is a natural reaction. Unfortunately for the parent the child continues to live with, he will usually be most comfortable ventilating his anger toward *her.* It is generally much more threatening to tell the parent who left "I'm mad at you," since the child will be afraid that even less contact may be the result.

page 6: Mommy and Daddy say they know how I feel. They have mad and sad feelings, too, but we need to try to plan together what is best for us all.

The main way that children learn that their feelings can be accepted and shared is for parents to share their own similar feelings. Parents can tell their children about how they are feeling, as long as an effort is made to avoid blaming ("I'm mad at your Mommy, too. She really is a louse for leaving us"). Children need to understand that being mad is part of the hurt that is involved in missing someone. A father might say: "I feel mad, too, about Mommy leaving, sometimes I just miss her. I'm sorry that we couldn't work things out."

Even when children and parents are angry about what has happened, an effort should be made to continue a spirit of cooperation, supporting the continued growth of each family member. When parents can maintain some ability to communicate and share ideas about what may be most helpful for their children, they will benefit as much as their children. Those children will learn that people can manage to get along, even when there are differences.

page 7: Mommy and Daddy say that they are getting a divorce from being a husband and wife. But you can't get a divorce from being a Mommy or a Daddy. They will always be my Mommy and Daddy.

Just as children can be reassured by a spirit of cooperation and communication between separating parents, they enjoy being reminded that mothers and fathers have a parenting job to do that is not dependent upon the marriage. Children need a lot of reassurance, especially during the breakup of their families. They need to be reminded that their needs will still be met, that they will be kept safe, and that they are still loved by both parents. This message needs to be continuously reinforced.

Children are also made vulnerable by their own anger toward each parent. When you are angry with someone, you naturally feel less secure in that relationship. It is even harder when you do not feel safe enough to mention that anger. Children may, as a result, spend a lot of time asking for reassurance and/or contact, when they are actually angry.

It may be useful to reassure the child as you question: "You know I really love you and that you really love me. But sometimes we can get mad at each other. I know that Mommy and Daddy not living together anymore has made you a little mad. Don't you feel a little mad at me, too?"

This type of question tells the child that the parent is prepared to have the child say, "Yes, I'm mad," and won't become defensive or make excuses. But if the emotional atmosphere is too tense, such questions and statements are generally useless. Children are strongly affected by their immediate perceptions of the emotional atmosphere, and they will not believe it is safe or possible to give an honest answer. They will tell you what they think you want to hear, rather than expose another point of tension.

page 8: Sometimes I get mixed up about what is going on and why Mommy and Daddy are so sad and mad.

Emotional tension affects everyone's ability to make sense of experiences. For both parents and children, knowing that what you perceive is real, not imagined, can make you feel better. Once the sources of tension are acknowledged, parents can help children to feel less mixed up. Children can be told that sometimes mothers and fathers feel really bad and cannot control their words or their actions well. And they can be reassured that adults will try, just as kids have to do. But often children witness one parent or the other acting badly, for example, while they are being dropped off or picked up for visits. Children will manage such confusion most easily when both parents can admit that their emotions or behavior may be "hard to boss" from time to time.

page 9: Mommy and Daddy told me that we can make extra
pages for my book as helpers when I get mixed up
and ask questions.

Children can be greatly helped by having a Daddy who can
explain Mommy's plans and point of view, and a Mommy who
can explain Daddy's, in a positive and reasonable way without
projecting blame. This does not mean that parents have to
rubber-stamp all of each other's ideas, just that respect and
understanding is extended for and by both.

page 10: Daddy said we can talk about the pages when we
visit.

This page emphasizes the fact that when children are
comfortable in their relationships with both parents, they will
want talk to each about the other. Such communication can be
closed off when exchanges between the parents lead the child
to feel that there is a reputation war going on. Later on, a child
may learn how to exploit or manipulate such situations for his
own ends, but most younger children will simply shut down at
this point. When a pattern of managing emotional conflict by
keeping some experiences isolated and secret evolves, the
child's emotional development can be damaged.

page 11: It made me sad that Mommy and Daddy do not want
to live together. But I still have both my Mommy
and my Daddy. Now I have two special places to
call my home.

The bright side—"now I have two homes"—can be conveyed
as an opportunity, not just a burden. As the transition to a two-
home family evolves, more positive information can be
included, showing how the child's world has expanded. The
book can begin to include the different approaches and
experiences that each parent has to offer.

All too often, parents experience too much bitterness during
separation to collaborate in the fashion suggested above.

The sad reality is that when husbands leave their wives, or vice-versa, the departing parent often *does* eventually divorce the children as well, through gradually decreasing contact and even failure to continue support payments. The implications of such possibilities call for another version of "When Mommy and Daddy Got Divorced."

Daddy Said Goodbye

page 1: Daddy said goodbye last week. He kind of forgot to tell me and my sister. Mommy said Daddies sometimes get mixed up about what to say, but we can try to talk about what happened.

When divorce occurs precipitously or without clear communication, the child cannot be included in any kind of planned sharing. Often, in such situations, patterns of reasonable communication have never been established within the family. This separation, then, becomes an opportunity for the remaining parent to begin to establish such patterns. If so, it is important to tell the child that, in their family, people have generally "kind of forgotten to talk things over."

While it may be difficult to do, new patterns of exchange within the family are best begun in a spirit that avoids recriminations. People can be forgiven for a failure to talk things over; a new start can be made. A page could include some (nonblaming) discussion of what things were like in the family before Daddy left.

page 2: Mommy says we're a new kind of family now. We're a divorced family. That means that the Mommy and Daddy don't live together in the same house. Mommy gets to stay with the kids.

In a single-parent family, as in any other, there is a need to share information, and, when resources are stretched, there is less adult time. Clarity about schedules, chores, and cooperation are required for smooth family functioning. Some studies have shown that children in single-parent homes have gained a sense of independence and self-reliance that serves them well in later life. If these skills are associated with an ability to share information and feelings, children of divorce can be doubly advantaged in their future interpersonal relationships, if their sense of trust has not been damaged.

page 3: We feel sad and mad and mixed-up. I liked Daddy here, except when he and Mommy would fight. That would make me sad and scared. Mommy said it's okay to talk about it.

Talking is an important way to relieve the stress that children in this situation are bound to feel, but a period of turmoil and adjustment should still be expected. During a time when uncertainty affects the adults involved, children will certainly feel at least as sad, mad, and mixed-up, and no purpose is served by denying that fact. And however confused and disturbed the remaining parent may be, she is still in charge. Her confusion should not be presented as a plea to the children to take over. Limits still need to be set. At times of stress, while children may test them more, it is extremely reassuring for them to have those limits.

The attachment to the father also needs to be stated, even in those cases where he was already a peripheral member of the household. The child deserves the opportunity to hold onto some memories that contribute to comfort. That attachment, however, does not have to be built on falsehoods. If Daddy and Mommy fought, if Daddy was previously disappointing or angry, the book can remind the child that this was indeed the case. It does not necessarily contradict the fact that the child liked his Daddy.

Mommy and the child can talk about Daddy, about what was, what is today, and the uncertainty surrounding what happens tomorrow. Children can accept that something may be uncertain, as long as they feel that a parent is still trying to figure out what is best for everybody. Their anxiety is further diminished by the ability to talk about what might happen next.

> page 4: Mommy is really mad at Daddy. We don't know what Daddy thinks yet, but Mommy said he won't be home for a while.

In such situations, it is not harmful for the child to know that Mommy is mad about Daddy's departure. Even in relationships in which there was little comfort or stability, no one likes to be abandoned, and the child will be aware of these feelings. Even the most careful parent cannot shield her child from the nonverbal messages and the occasional conversations with friends and family where she expresses how she feels. The child should, however, be reassured that Mommy's feelings won't prohibit him from talking with Daddy, or from learning his plans.

> page 5: When Daddy knows what his plans are, Mommy said she would tell us and maybe we can talk to Daddy on the phone.

The child needs to know that a relationship with the father can continue, if at all possible. Sometimes a caretaking parent will need the support of a therapeutic relationship, so that communication with the children is not distorted or confused by her own feelings. In rare cases, communication between a separated parent and a child can be so bitter that it undermines the child's stability and security. Then both counseling and legal action may be called for. The story can be modified accordingly.

> page 6: Sometimes when I go to school I get grouchy or feel sad and cry. I just think about my family. My teacher says I can tell her about my worries.

Most children also need to be reminded that other adults in their life can understand their feelings and help them to get through them. Children under any form of stress are likely to experience episodes of tearfulness and withdrawal, or to show anger and anxiety in interactions with peers. They will be tempted to share their feelings with a special teacher. Teachers are extremely important people in children's lives. Parents should inform teachers about potential stress, and children should be given permission to talk about what they are feeling, since no young child (and few adults) have the ability to completely cover up their own unhappiness or anger.

page 7: Mommy says we can still be a happy family. We can help each other out. We can talk about our feelings. We can make a calendar of the fun things we can do.

The reassurance that the family can continue to be happy should be stated. Yes, there will still be bad moments, but the spirit of a positive family life can be stressed. Sharing and cooperation can be reinforced. Even in the busiest family, a special time for talking can be set aside and marked on the calendar, or for reading a book or watching a program together, or for a walk to a neighborhood playground on a weekend.

page 8: Our family is different now. Sometimes I miss my Daddy. But here are pictures of all the other special grown-ups who love me and help our family.

While there will be differences, the new family unit can practice all the things that contribute to the developing strengths of children: the ability to share, honesty and dialogue, responsibility for self and consideration of others, self-discipline, and the cultivation of love. These attributes can be seen in the larger family network of relatives and friends, and the child can be reminded that to be a child of divorce is not to be alone or lonely. While children will feel the pain of divorce and the concurrent disruption of previously established modes of family functioning, they can still learn positive ways to take care of themselves and to relate to others.

< **9** >

Stories About Adoption and Parental Injury

Children can both understand and accept the simple fact of adoption. It does not need to be an emotionally charged or negative piece of information. It can seem as natural as having freckles. But some attention must be paid to creating an atmosphere that permits children to express their feelings and questions about the topic. A homemade book can help, but parents need to be able to accept, and to answer, the adopted child's further questions. If these generate anxiety in the parent's mind, the child will detect this. The child's acceptance of the situation is predicated upon prior acceptance by the parents.

A Book About Me: How I Got Adopted

page 1: My name is _____.
I live at _____.
I live with _____.
They love me very much. I love them and give them hugs and say, "I love you."

Children should be introduced to the fact that they were adopted *before* they begin school. Children who learn this fact later in life, outside the home, always experience a great sense of dismay and confusion. This can undermine the love and trust that had been established between the adoptive parents and the child.

page 2: But I didn't always live here.
         Once I lived in _____.
         I had another Mommy and Daddy.
         They loved me very much and decided to make me so
              I could have a special time in the world.

This experience of the past, no matter how brief, offers a sense of time and place. A birthplace defines a little piece of each person's identity, even if they did not live there long enough to have any memories. If you ask people where they are from, they often say something like, "I grew up in New York, but I was born in Philadelphia." Information about the child's birth does not diminish the strength or importance of the bond between adoptive parents and the child. It is simply a part of their identity.

Adopted children must also find a place for their birth parents in their hearts and minds. If children are to acquire that fundamental acceptance of the gift of life that helps people endure tribulations on this planet, they need to understand that they were conceived in "love" (we are all accidents, to some extent, of time and whim). On this most basic level, children need to be reassured that their biological parents wanted a life for them, if they are going to take their lives seriously enough to struggle with the pain of existence, even while they permit themselves to accept its joys.

page 3: One day my first Mommy and Daddy said, "We can't do the job of parents. It's too hard. Let's see if we can find a helper." And they did. There are special helpers who help babies (and little boys and girls) to find new parents to love them and help them grow up. They found me my new family.

Children can accept that some mothers and fathers cannot take care of kids; they know it is a big job. They can be helped to appreciate that their first parents wanted their child to be cared for in ways that they themselves were unable to provide.

page 4: After I finish reading this book as much as I want, we can put it in the special box that has my other special papers. Mommy and Daddy keep them safe for me, just as they keep me safe now.

Making this book for a child and sharing it over a period of time allows her to accept and assimilate the information you are providing. There is no major discussion of feelings in this little book, just a statement of the love that both birth parents and foster parents feel for the child. This basic information about adoption is not anxiety provoking, nor should it create any special sadness or anger, unless there are other family issues affecting the child. If she persists in asking questions, it may be a clue that she, or the family, needs some extra help from a professional.

For most children, though, once this book becomes familiar, the story will not be needed any longer and should be put in that "special safe place" with the other papers that parents keep for their children. The issue is put away, too. It will be there for the child to review at some later time, but does not require a great deal of ongoing reflection. It is just a simple fact of life, like the love and acceptance that exists within the adoptive family.

Some children may have had a more extensive history of placements with families; occasionally, children are placed with a foster family, then returned to a biological parent, then removed again. If this is the case, you may need some additional guidance about how to modify this book (see Chapter 5). For some children, it is important to include all this information in a simple and straightforward way. For example:

page 5: My mommy asked for help to take care of me. Helpers found me a new home. It was in _____.
page 6: Then, Mommy thought she could take care of me

again, so I went to live with her. It was too hard. Mommy's helpers found me a new home.

page 7: Now that I am _____ years old, I live with the _____ family. Mommy, my helpers, and the rest of my family have all made a deal so that I can live here until I get to be big.

That last piece of information is shared with the understanding that children are vulnerable to anxiety associated with any shifts of living situation, and will need reassurance that a stable "deal" has been made. In any instances where that is not the case, professional guidance should be sought for the child while such issues are still in flux.

Another story is included here. It was written for Andrew, a child who had recently lost both his grandmother to death, and his father to the ravages of alcoholism. The story's title, "Sometimes It's a Sad Life," is drawn from the four-year-old boy's comments during his visit with me. As in Andrew's case, the greatest danger children face is in having to isolate their feelings and their observations about what is happening around them. Children can adapt to a great many different types of realities when they are permitted to understand and express what they feel. Making this information into stories children can share with a parent can help them a great deal. They can be helped to understand many different life predicaments, within the context of a loving and honest relationship.

Sometimes It's a Sad Life

page 1: First Nana left. She got sick. She had to go to God.

page 2: Then Dad got sick from alcohol. He couldn't boss himself with alcohol. He left home to go to the hospital.

page 3: Now Mommy and Daddy don't live together. They couldn't make a deal. A "deal" is when two people agree that the same thing is a good idea.

The facts are stated simply and acknowledge that this story is not a happy one. The story goes on to suggest ways the child can cope with these difficult problems. It never suggests that the sadness and hurt, and sometimes anger, will go away, since the realities of a disrupted family life do not.

page 4: Sometimes I miss my Dad. I feel sad. Dr. Bob told me it was OK to cry because sometimes things are sad.

It is important to remind children that sadness is a natural response to difficult life situations. It is helpful to remind them that it is all right to cry. The wish to be "brave" can distort a child's emotional development.

page 5: Sometimes I feel mad because Mom and Dad couldn't make a deal. Mom and Dad are mad at each other, too.

Children will often feel angry when parents separate. The idea of "not making a deal" avoids blaming either parent. Even when one parent is, in fact, more responsible for the separation, it does not help the child to assign blame. The child will also hear, in one way or another, the parents' hurt or anger with each other. It can be admitted openly.

page 6: Mom and Dad still love me. Sometimes I feel mad anyway. I wish I could chase all the baddies away.

Parents need to remember that love, in the short run, does not make everything better. It still hurts. In the long run, of course, the child's sense of parental love and support does help. In Andrew's case, his fantasy play was full of fights with "baddies" (as is normal for four-year-olds). In this case, "baddies" becomes a metaphor for unhappy events and feelings.

page 7: I still talk to Daddy on the telephone at night.
page 8: I still go to daycare and play with my friends. We like to play turtles.

page 9:   I still live at home with Mommy and have my own
          room.
page 10: I still like to watch my special shows on TV and play
          games.
page 11: I am still learning lots of big boy things. I can even
          put together the hard snaps on my overalls. I
          still can't take them apart, but I will soon.
page 12: PROUD LIST:

   These pages reinforce a sense of security. Although the
family is different and some feelings are troublesome, many
things are still the same. The child's Proud List emphasizes
that competence and self-sufficiency will still be mastered.

   Many of the concerns that children have relate as much to
their worries about their parents' feelings as they do to their
own, because they realize that their parents can not help them
while they themselves are still in turmoil. When parents are
overwhelmed, children may need to distance themselves in
order to come to terms with their own feelings. The more
aware the parents are of their own position, the more receptive they can be to their children's different feelings and
understanding.
   Too often, kids wind up as receptacles for their parents'
unresolved feelings. And frequently, when children are
brought to therapy, it is their parents who are most in need
of it.

PARENTAL INJURY OR DISABILITY

   Even though it sometimes took second place to the other
information presented, defining and managing feelings
has been the point of nearly every book described so far. In
Chapter 7, where we discussed helping youngsters to manage
an illness, their feelings were central. When a child has to
cope with the illness of a parent, a special friend, or a close
relative, her own feelings become an even more important
part of what she must recognize and think about.

This next book deals with the impact on a family of a serious accident, where children will have to manage a range of emotions. First is fear: Why did it happen? Will it happen again? Like the survivors of plane crashes or earthquakes, children may wonder if there is some basic flaw in the ordered universe they have just begun to know. When the unexpected happens, anxiety can make established routines more difficult to follow, and there may be a general regression in behavior, reviving fears that characterized an earlier developmental phase.

Next is anger. It is very important to remember that children have complex feelings about their parents. They can see them as a source of frustration as well as of love. And they can feel a great deal of anger toward them, even in normal circumstances. Sometimes, at a stage when a child has been showing more independence, or when the parent's own behavior provokes ambivalence (for example, by being particularly strict or unpredictable), anger can make a child wonder if *her* own bad feelings or wishes have somehow caused whatever terrible thing happened to the parent. Much of this guilt may be unconscious, but the child will guard against the other parent or anyone else learning of it. Professional help may be necessary to sort out these complicated feelings.

In addition to that guilty sort of anger, children can be mad at the cause of the accident, at the parent who was hurt (Why did he make such an awful mistake?), and at the parent remaining (Why didn't she protect him?). Anger is a common part of all human experience, but adults have had more opportunities to learn how to manage it, and their sense of time is much more realistic. For children, the waiting (for Mommy or Daddy to be well again) often seems endless.

But anger can also serve as a protection from fear. Children can become more demanding and irritable. They want to test whether their world can still be the way it was before. They worry about never being able to get a piggyback ride again. The more such reactions can be labeled and connected to what happened, the less distress the child will feel.

In "Daddy's Accident," the beginning of the story defines what an accident is: something that you don't want to have happen, but it does happen, anyway. This definition covers everything from spilled milk and other "mess-ups" that all kids know about to real disasters. The particular circumstances can be discussed in a simple way.

The sadness that is part of any trauma is described on a page devoted to the fact that everybody cries, sometimes. In a home where open communication has been fostered, children will ask, "Why are you crying so much?" They will need gentle reminders that grown-ups can feel sad and worried when something bad happens. The parent can remind the child of times when she felt badly, and reassure her that everyone will, little by little, feel better.

Experiencing trauma prompts a lot of fantasizing. The child can imagine all sorts of things that might have happened to prevent the accident. Her mind can be full of wishes, revising the past, present, or future. Fantasies can help her to escape from the pain and sense of loss. They can also lead to long-term goals. Many children whose families endured serious illnesses will, later on, go into medicine or other helping professions.

Again, as in all our storybooks, the child should be kept informed of all basic details of what is happening. Visits to the hospital should be should be discussed. It also helps if children can meet a doctor or nurse who is caring for the ill parent.

"Daddy's Accident" was written for two children, four and five years old. The father in this family was particularly stern, as well as somewhat unpredictable in his behavior toward his children, who were aware that they did not always like him. Ambivalence is something children can begin to understand by the age of three or four. They can learn that sometimes you get mad at Daddy, and sometimes you love him, just as sometimes you like to play with your friends, and sometimes you don't. Ambivalence is defined here so that guilt does not complicate the child's grieving too much. However, in some cases professional guidance may be necessary.

Daddy's Accident

page 1:   One day, when Daddy was driving, he had an accident. An accident is something that you don't want to happen, that does happen.

page 2:   A grown-up had made a terrible mistake. It hurt my daddy. It made us scared. We felt mad and sad. When I make a mistake, I get yelled at. Who yells at grown-ups?

page 3:   Daddy was badly hurt. His head was banged and he had to go to the hospital. If only Daddy had been in a different place, he might not have been hurt. We felt mad and bad.

page 4:   Mommy cried. We all cried. Daddy cried, too.

page 5:   Wouldn't it be nice to make sure there was never another accident. Maybe everyone could learn to do things right, or a machine could be invented to stop fast cars.

page 6:   I wish bad things didn't have to happen, then I wouldn't have to feel bad.

page 7:   Now my daddy stays at the hospital. Mommy visits him.

page 8:   Things are very busy at home. When Mommy comes home from the hospital, she tells us about Daddy. We still feel very sad.

page 9:   When Daddy was home, he helped us remember the rules. Now that he is in the hospital, Mommy has to help us remember them. Daddy said rules help us to be big boys.

page 10: Sometimes we got mad about the rules. They can be hard to follow. But we can try to help each other out.

page 11: Daddy is getting better, but he is still hurt. We are still mad and sad and scared.

page 12: But Mommy tells us that we are still a family, and we will talk about our feelings and do things as a family.

DADDY'S ACCIDENT

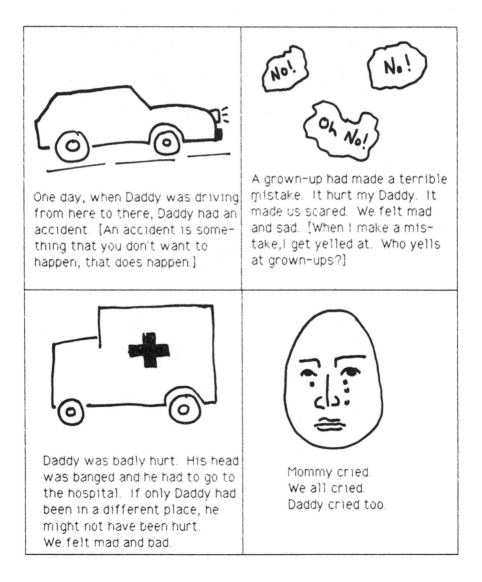

One day, when Daddy was driving from here to there, Daddy had an accident. [An accident is something that you don't want to happen, that does happen.]

A grown-up had made a terrible mistake. It hurt my Daddy. It made us scared. We felt mad and sad. [When I make a mistake, I get yelled at. Who yells at grown-ups?]

Daddy was badly hurt. His head was banged and he had to go to the hospital. If only Daddy had been in a different place, he might not have been hurt. We felt mad and bad.

Mommy cried.
We all cried.
Daddy cried too.

Wouldn't it be nice to make sure there was never another accident. Maybe everyone could learn to do things right, or a machine could be invented to stop fast cars.
I wish bad things didn't have to happen, then I wouldn't have to feel bad.

Now my Daddy stays at the hospital. Mommy visits him. Things are very busy at home. When Mommy comes home from the hospital, Mommy tells us about Daddy.
We still feel very sad.

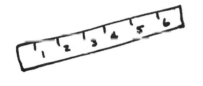

When Daddy was home, he helped us remember the rules. Now that Daddy is in the hospital, Mom has to help us remember the rules. Daddy said rules helped us to be big boys.
Sometimes we got mad about the rules. They can be hard to follow. But we can try and help each other out.

Daddy is getting better but he is still hurt. We are still mad and sad and scared. But Mommy tells us that we are still a family and we will talk about our feelings and do things as a family.

Daddy's Accident: Part II

page 1:   One day our Daddy had an accident. It was a bad accident. So bad, we worried that Daddy might die. But he didn't. Now he's getting well.

page 2:   Daddy used to go to the office a lot. He was a big boss. When he came home, he liked things just so. He bossed us, too. He made us a little scared and mad. But we tried to do just what he said. We made mistakes that would make Daddy mad.

page 3:   Now Daddy is still at the hospital. But he is different. Sometimes he gets mad easily and is very bossy. Sometimes he says sad things. Sometimes it is hard to understand him. We get mixed up.

page 4:   Our old Daddy is like a new Daddy. He can't walk. His words don't always work. He gets things mixed up, too. It makes us feel bad.

page 5:   Daddy's accident hurt his brain. Your brain is the boss of the messages to your body. You can get it to send a message to your toe. You can get the brain to say, "Hello, toe, wiggle!" And, it will.

page 6:   Daddy's brain got hurt so that it doesn't send messages very easily to his arm and his leg. Sometimes Daddy can't get his brain to talk right. He can't get it to help him with his feelings. He feels scared and sad and mad, too, just like us. But we can talk about our feelings with Mommy.

page 7:   Sometimes Mommy gets so worried about Daddy and all the jobs she has to do that she gets mad easily. She tells us to go to our room!

page 8:   Later on she tells us that she loves us and that things are hard. We feel sad.

page 9:   It's hard having a Daddy that's not like the old Daddy. His body and his brain are still trying to get well. It takes a long time.

page 10: We have gotten used to the new way things are in our family. Sometimes we still feel sad and mad about it, but we love each other, too.

By the time the second part of "Daddy's Accident" was written (eight months after the first part), the extent of the father's brain damage was better understood. He was a different man and would be a different Daddy. The more a parent's personality or physical abilities are altered by injury or illness, the more the children will be affected, and the more help they will need to understand what the impact might be on their interactions with that parent and on family routines. For instance, when someone has suffered a heart attack, there may be nothing different that a child can see, but that adult may be less able to play vigorously or to climb stairs for a bedtime kiss.

Another sort of change that needs to be clarified is how the structure of the family may be altered. In cases of severe trauma, it can be transformed, functionally, into a one-parent household. Whatever support the other parent provided will now be absent, and the remaining parent will necessarily be less available. In this sense, illness within the family presents the same problems for children as divorce. They often feel as if they have lost both parents. Understanding which elements of the situation particularly affect *your* child will help you to shape the content of the books you make.

"No More Hospitals!" was written for a younger child. Here the medical situation was of less concern than the fact of multiple separations from his mother. The comings and goings of various caretakers was also confusing and anxiety provoking. The child's dismay was focused on the hospitals in order to give him an opportunity to be mad at something other than his parents.

No More Hospitals!
A Book about Willy and His Family

page 1: First Mommy had to go to the hospital to bring home a new baby. The new baby came home with her. That was okay, I guess. She did get a lot of attention, but I got to be a big brother. I could hold her and do lots of things that she couldn't do. Daddy told me that I was really a big boy.

page 2: But when Mommy was in the hospital getting that baby, it was busy here. Daddy was only home in the mornings and at night. I went to Grandma and Grandpa's house. One day they took me to the hospital to see the new baby and Mommy.

page 3: Other people (pictures provided) helped take care of me. I got to play a lot with my friend Harry at his house. Then, when the new baby (her name is Lila) was starting to look around, and I was just getting used to my new nursery school...

page 4: Mommy had to go to the hospital again for tests. What are tests? That's when doctors check your body to see that everything is okay. It meant that it got busy here all over again. Paula came, and then Aunt Emily came to help take care of us. My friend Sara came over a lot with her Daddy.

page 5: Daddy and Mommy seemed a little worried. Everybody felt a little sad. Then the doctors (they should stay in their offices) told us that Mommy had to go back to the hospital again.

page 6: OH, NO! I thought, NO MORE HOSPITALS! But Mommy and Daddy said the doctors were trying to be helpers. They had to help Mommy and her body to get well. She had a no-good lump that they had to take away.

page 7: But while Mommy is in the hospital this time (the THIRD time), we'll be busy again. Aunt Emily, Uncle Charlie, Cousin Rachel, and Cousin Jonah will be here. Other grown-ups will help, too. I'll play with my cousins and with my friend, Harry. Daddy will still be home sometimes. I'll still go to school.

page 8: Then MOMMY WILL BE HOME AGAIN!

page 9: Daddy tells me that Mommy will be tired and in bed a lot. She won't be able to pick me up. She'll be

happy to be with me and with Lila and Daddy.
We'll be happy, too.
page 10: When Mommy comes home again, we'll read this
book together and say, NO MORE HOSPITALS!

Because "No More Hospitals" was written for a three-year-old, the child's feelings are not emphasized to the same degree as they might be for a child of four or five. A child this young is still in the process of labeling feelings and needs more immediate comforting and contact. As she develops more cognitive ability, descriptions of circumstances evoking certain emotions will be more comprehensible. As with much of parenting, trial and error may be necessary. Some children may be ready to hear more about feelings at an earlier age than others. Your child's current reactions will tell you how much, and in what way, feelings should be emphasized.

Children, as we all know, are nothing if not different. Some are more tearful, worried, or scared about a host of life experiences. Others may be mad a lot of the time, or show aggression much more readily. Throughout your child's development, even while taking into account such predispositions, it is important to help her to achieve a sense of balance. Angry-acting children must learn that sometimes they are actually scared or jealous. They need to develop a capacity for managing their frustration with words rather than actions. Sad children must work on being able to stick up for themselves. Anxious children must attempt to manage life's adventures so that they can consolidate a sense of pride.

The books you write should incorporate what you know about your child's particular style, as well as what you hope she will learn. Since the books are your own creations, the way your child feels can be described in ways she is already familiar with, using her particular vocabulary. Once you have helped her to be better prepared for whatever specific events might be troubling her, you can turn to other, more general stories, to help her to realize that other kids have to cope with difficult problems, too.

< **10** >

New Endings for Old Stories

Homemade books can commemorate a special achievement or review a special experience (such as completing a year at a new school); they can also help to break the roles that sometimes evolve for children within their families. The "serious" child can be shown in moments of laughter; the "clumsy" one can be portrayed in an especially adept moment; the "bad" one can be shown doing something considerate.

It is always amazing to me how quickly and indelibly kids can be typecast within a family. While much has been written about constricting roles in alcoholic or dysfunctional families, or ones with handicapped children, they often occur in average families, too. These roles soon shape how the child defines himself and influence his motivation to be otherwise. "What do I care? They'll just think I'm stupid, anyway." A cycle of self-defeating behavior can take over.

But parents can break into this cycle, if they are willing to open up and take a new look at their child's behavior and see how varied it truly is. Our minds like to simplify what we see, but children are complex creatures. The key to their future success (our own, as well) lies in the ability to adapt to new and changing circumstances. We should want our children to feel comfortable with as many different talents and sides of their personalities as possible.

Roles that constrict aspects of personality development are only one sort of hazard within the family. Another relates to

how parents accept their child's temperamental character-
istics (activity level, range of moods) and cognitive style (the
ways a child learns about life, for instance, how he uses his
body to experience and explore things—or just sits there,
fantasizing). Too often, we say things like "He's such a wonderful little boy, I don't know how he can do such malicious
things!" rather than "Johnny works so hard to be good. He
must get angry sometimes, too. But unless he makes a really
big mistake, he has trouble showing it."

The more some aspect of anyone's personality is labeled
"insecure," "nasty," or "intolerable," the more it is likely to be
put into action, rather than thought about. And the more some
part of our emotions or our behavior gets cut off from conscious
review in childhood, the more risk there is of our lives feeling
out of control when we are adults. One facet of the self should
not be shut off from the others. If we cannot get in touch with
our anger, we cannot be reasonably assertive. If we are
convinced we are clumsy, it is harder to attempt new tasks that
require physical effort. Insecurity, compounded by negative
parental attitudes, diminishes our inner resources.

Parents can make books about various aspects of a child's
style (without calling it good or bad) that can help him to
accept himself more comfortably. These books are a way to
discuss his shortcomings without negative labels. A good
starting point can be any moment when the child shows he can
be different, or whenever he attempts something new. If you
are worried about his temper, choose a time when he has done
a good job of sharing or has tolerated frustration without the
usual outburst. If you are concerned that a child is too clumsy,
pick an instance of successful coordination, or emphasize how
well he has been doing lately at *not* dropping things, as in "I
Didn't Drop My Wheaties Today." If you feel he lacks athletic
prowess, support his try at something new, as in "Guess Who
Joined the Swim Team."

In these two following examples, notice: 1) the accepting
description of the child's behavior; 2) the effort to commend
the child's awareness of the difficulty and attempts to change;
and 3) the credit given when the child is able to do something

new. (It is also possible to include how the family has tried to help and how support and recognition can be offered to all.)

I Didn't Drop My Wheaties Today

page 1: Everyday we all have breakfast. Everybody in the family has a morning job. Mom and Dad, Katie, and Jim all bring their bowls to the table. I like to fill up my bowl at the counter. I like a lot of Wheaties.

page 2: Jimmy always says, "Look at Timmy's Wheaties trail." Kate tries to make me laugh. Once I dropped the whole bowl. Mom and Dad say, "Bring the box to the table." I don't like to do that. Sometimes Dad tells me that if I spill my Wheaties one more time, I'll have to eat Corn Flakes.

page 3: Mom told me I was a good cleaner-upper. She lets our dog help me out. Sometimes I cry because, by the time I get to the table, everybody else is ready to leave, and I feel lonely. Mom says, "It's too bad you spill your Wheaties, and that makes you late."

page 4: Today, I filled my bowl at the counter. The Wheaties made a big mountain on top, and I could see an avalanche beginning to slide off the edge, so I put my bowl back on the counter and put some Wheaties back in the box. Then I went to the table.

page 5: Everybody said, "There's no Wheaties trail today."
page 6: I didn't spill my Wheaties today!

We all want our children to succeed, but success is usually neither immediate or magical. Studies have shown that people who do well have the capacity to persist and to tolerate frustration. Occasional failure is the price of progress, but some children seem to face more than occasional defeat. Consider the child whose skills with a ball are more like a bird's than a seal's. Birds have wonderful qualities, but if they had to go into a gym everyday and play dodgeball, they might lose their ability to fly! What can save a child like that is a spirit of persistence that waits for another activity to come along.

Trying something new means tolerating the idea (and the fact and the feelings) of failure. While the popular saying tells us that "it is better to try and fail than never to have tried at all," children often need a great deal of support to be able to keep on trying after repeated failures.

High achievement often reflects continuous effort and a steady sense of self-esteem. How parents help their children to deal with attempting new things and surviving disappointment is an essential aspect of their success. Children need to be able to consider what is hard and what is easy for them. They need to learn to distinguish between skills that develop naturally for them and the ones requiring more practice. Making this distinction helps children take the next step: understanding what affected their performance and what they can do to improve on it.

Some things, though, will always be difficult. Children need to realize that not doing well at certain activities does not mean that they should not try others. Even perfectionists have to admit that no one can be the best at everything. Life involves searching for what matches our talents and temperaments. Success is then learning, and persisting in, whatever makes that match work as well as possible.

Trying something new means taking risks, and children sometimes experience each new attempt as an overwhelming ordeal. For some youngsters, this feeling can become focused on sports. Physical activity and games are part of every child's life almost from infancy, and positive early experiences can contribute to sound attitudes about fairness, achievement, motivation, and assertiveness, as well as fitness and health. But sports can also make some children feel unduly pressured and unsuccessful in activities or at levels of performance that are truly beyond their capacities.

This next book was written for a child whose first love was reading, to help confirm her sense of herself as a competing athlete nevertheless.

Guess Who Joined the Swim Team

page 1: Here are pictures of Kate in her early sports ventures. This is the hopscotch court she and Allison drew on the blacktopped driveway.

page 2: And this is our neighborhood basketball court, where she used to meet her friends and play, until Timmy started to come along, and always got the ball in faster than she did when everyone was playing Around the World.

page 3: Kate used to feel that reading was her favorite activity. Jimmy would say that she had the fastest index finger in town, and Dad used to do finger pushups when she was late for supper because she "just wanted to finish the chapter."

page 4: Here's a list of some of the most wonderful books she's read, and her school award for readership.

page 5: Kate used to go to a pool with her nursery school class, and everyone called her "the fish." But when Kate was six, she just hated it when her hair got wet, and she wouldn't swim anymore.

page 6: When she went to middle school this year, one gym choice was swimming. Kate took it because the only other winter choice was basketball. Mom and Dad got her a hair dryer to keep in her school locker. She saved the warranty—here it is.

page 7: After her gym class in swimming was over, Kate's gym teacher asked her to join the team in the spring. She said no.

page 8: Mom and Dad talked about how she was a really good swimmer when she was little—they even looked at the old pictures together.

page 9: Dad made a deal with Kate that if she went to the Y swim program to see if she could learn some more strokes, he'd get her a new book she wanted. Kate agreed, and the Y teacher said she was the fastest back-stroke student at the Y in two years.

page 10:   When Kate came home from school the next day, she was down to supper on time. She had a little smile on her face and was very quiet. Finally Mom said, "What's up?" Kate just said, "Guess who joined the swim team?"

< **11** >

What to Do if Your Child Hates the Book

First of all, expect your child to love her homemade book. Most kids do. These stories tell them something about their own world. The books help them to organize their ideas and feelings about a little slice of life in an enjoyable way, making them less anxious about whatever is going on. Even if your child has never seemed anxious, you may hear a sigh of relief when you share a story you have written for her. Little children do worry about changes. And they enjoy learning that Mommy and Daddy are thinking about their world. They like stories!

Second, don't be discouraged if your child doesn't like the book right away. Her worries may be somewhat greater than you thought, and the story may bring it all to the forefront. Lay back. Leave the book around. See what happens. Make it a choice for storytime a few days later. In the meantime, ask her some questions about the change or event described in the book. She may be able to tell you more specifically what is needed to make the story work better.

Third, ask someone else to read the story to her. If this is your first endeavor, it may be that your child is concerned about you! Children are very sensitive to parents' tensions and nonverbal messages. Give yourself a break, and see if somebody else can help you out.

Here are some other things to consider:

Make sure that your child understands the book.

The first thing to do is to play a naming game with the pictures. Can your child name the cast of characters in the book? If it is about the family, most one- to two-year-olds can do this, even with stick figures. Once you have labeled them for her, your child can use the visual cues of size, hair length, and items of clothing to identify them again. (Photos may be more helpful for the very young child; older children might prefer them, too.)

If the story is about an impending move, the child may need to warm up to the idea of travel. Get some other books about trucks and planes, and use the natural interest that preschool children have in big machines that make noise. Or cut out pictures showing other climates, to help her to get used to the fact that there are many kinds of places in the world. Curiosity is most kids' strong suit. Think about different ways to tap into it.

If the subject you are introducing is a new baby in the family, even if she is not happy about having a little sister or brother (kids are usually delighted), your child will be curious about babies in general. You can work on increasing her exposure to baby-related experiences.

The more the book can be used in association with concrete experiences, the better. If you are preparing your child for starting school or daycare, make sure you visit with her first, at a time when you can stay for a while, and then leave with her. Try not to couple that initial experience with her fears of being left alone there for an extended period of time. The same goes for doctors and hospitals. It is much nicer to find out about those places when you do not have to get a shot.

If your book is about illness, see whether your child can name the doctor, the nurse, and other concrete details. If not, dolls or a play-doctor kit can help her to develop a positive attitude toward medical personnel. Define them as helpers, and use that term often. Labeling policemen, storekeepers, and teachers as helpers, too, will help her to catch on to this category.

Children begin the process of categorizing quite early, usually with sets of opposites, such as male and female, yes and no, big and little. You can help by practicing some of the feeling categories, as well. Make a happy face, a sad face, and a mad one, and see if your child is willing to pin these faces onto different pages. This is a good way to discover what she is feeling.

Try to determine whether the story is missing the mark.

As discussed earlier, a child's concerns can be strikingly different from her parents', sometimes so different that it is hard for you to imagine what they are.

If your child is comfortable with you, and you are comfortable with the topic, try to make another book. This time, ask *her* to make up the pages. They may be quite disjointed, but that doesn't matter. Let her tell you all her ideas. Some may seem inappropriate or quite silly, but take them seriously and make the new pages.

You may need to break this process down into a number ofdifferent exchanges if the child's attention span allows only one page to get done at a sitting. Put the pages into a special folder, so that each time you return to the topic, the child will know you are saving them, and that you consider them important.

Maybe you can invite one of her friends to join you. Other children her age may tune into the problem more quickly than you can. Children sometimes speak in parables and metaphors that are hard for adults to understand.

Above all, do not be discouraged. Try to get a translation of what your child is telling you by talking over the story with other family members or your friends. These ideas can be incorporated into the next version of the story. Then you can see if the child can use the revision as a springboard to clearer communication about whatever inhibited her enjoyment of the first draft. By this time, all indicators should be pointing to "Go," and success should greet your next reading.

Understand that the child's feelings may be so strong that she cannot tolerate the topic.

Some stories that affect a child's feelings can take a while to adjust to. For instance, when children leave a favorite preschool for the summer, some have a very difficult time sitting still for the goodbye story. They need a slower, step-by-step approach, and a lot of support while struggling with all their sad, mad, and scared feelings about school ending and missing their friends and teachers.

It may be that your story does indeed make your child feel whatever has been bothering her, but she may have been trying to repress those feelings, putting them aside and trying not to think about them. If so, think about why she needs to hear this news now, even though she wishes "the story would go away." Are you asking her to try to deal with something that she may need more time on?

Besides serving as the vehicle through which a child can begin to understand a life change, a book may also serve as a "displacement object." This means that the child may get mad at the book itself for bringing up a troublesome topic, for instance, her parents' divorce or an illness. This can actually help her focus on what is bothering her, though. And hearing her say, "I don't want to read that dumb book!" or finding it later shredded into little pieces, will show you just how much the child hates going to the doctor, or the fact that Mommy and Daddy are not living together anymore. Then you can sympathize: "Nobody likes being sick" or "Having a Mommy and a Daddy who live in different places isn't fun." This may produce an opportunity for dialogue or further reflection, and the child's emotions won't remain closed off or denied.

If the topic is an urgent one, but painful to consider, give your child as much time as you possibly can to talk about her feelings. Ask questions. Describe your own feelings. Let her know that you understand that the book is about feelings that are hard to talk about. Remind her that it is an important job, though, and that you can do it together. Be patient. Children may need a lot of repetition, support, and comfort in order to approach an emotionally charged topic.

Each time your child rejects the book, calmly admit that the book is about something mad, sad, or scary: "I know it makes you feel bad. I feel bad, too, but we can sit together and talk about it." The more you can help your child know that you can tolerate and accept those difficult feelings, the easier it will be for her to share them. Little by little, she should begin to be more accepting of at least parts of the book.

Rather than trying to read the whole story, you might just have your child pick one or two pages to look at. That way the whole book will not overwhelm her. She can deal with the topic in smaller bits, and choose which ones to take first. With calm acceptance and persistence on the parents' part, it is rare for a child who needs to hear a story to refuse it forever.

If your child does remain resistant and angry, you will probably notice other signs of troublesome feelings and behavior. Some children are so affected by their feelings about a difficult life event that they do shut down. Then the skills of an experienced play therapist may be called for. Therapists can help a child to approach a difficult topic at a bearable rate, by using the supportive interventions they have been trained to make.

For most children, though, the stories that you make will be appreciated and enjoyed long after the event passes. Children will want to keep them as part of their own history, or they can be collected into a big book about life in your family. Whatever kinds of stories you write, homemade books will increase communication, understanding, and trust between yourself and your children. And this will help give your children a sturdy base from which to grow into competent and confident adults.